SECOND NATURE

The Story of a Naturalist's Garden

Susie White

Saraband

Published by Saraband
3 Clairmont Gardens
Glasgow, G3 7LW

ISBN: 9781915089915
ebook: 9781916812062

1 2 3 4 5 6 7 8 9 10

Printed and bound in Great Britain by Clays Ltd, Elcograf S.p.A.

MIX
Paper | Supporting
responsible forestry
FSC® C018072

Caution: handling and consuming some plants can induce severe
(even, in rare cases, fatal) reactions. Where occasionally reference
is made in these pages to reported medicinal properties of plants,
reactions of inviduals vary, and it is always recommended to consult
your physician before trying any plant yourself. Neither the author
nor the publisher can accept any liability for any adverse effects
caused by handling or consuming wild plants.

Contents

To Lucy and Rory

A Garden in the Valley

This is what the buzzard sees. The steep bank of wood-land in the valley below. River winding through fields of round backed sheep. A rabbit on the stony track. Bank vole hurrying to safety in the dry-stone wall. The many shapes and textures of plants in a garden. The figure of a woman straightening, shading her eyes with the back of her hand and gazing up.

It's the mewing that makes me look up, easing my back from gardening, hand to forehead as I watch flared wing tips, splayed tail, a head twisting sideways as the buzzard scans the valley. All year round I watch them, lifting off above the tree line of the wood on the hill, the males plunging in daring displays, as many as seven buzzards circling slow on summer thermals, the young in August crying with croaky immature voices.

I imagine that I'm as familiar to them as they are to me. Studies show that birds can recognise people's faces and that's certainly true of the female tawny owl. Perched by day on a branch near the owl box containing her chick, she doesn't move as I scratch-scratch the path with my rake or when I pick early morning flowers. Yet she retreats deep into an ash tree when anyone else comes by.

Every day, there is something to note in my diary, a favourite black Moleskin with silky paper where the daily records go. It's partly that this little valley in the North Pennines is full of wildlife, partly that our garden has become a hub, a distillation of so many insects, mammals, songbirds, amphibians, reptiles and raptors. We've made this garden in response to the surrounding landscape, but also in imitation of its many layers and varied habitats. It's where habitats meet that there is particular richness of species and the garden is an attempt to emulate this diversity within its walls. Fourteen years ago, there was nothing here, just a bulldozed rectangle of compacted worm-less earth.

With my husband David, I'd often walked past this house and thought what a special place it was. It sits low beside the river East Allen, its simple double fronted shape – three windows above, one on either side of the front door – more perfect for a slight lack of symmetry between the two sides. The roof of stone slabs is a shade darker than the sandstone of the walls, and with a chimney at each end there's a sense of balance and calm. The door is edged by huge quoin stones and topped with a heavy lintel, hinting at its age.

As with all potential gardens, my mind transformed the weedy, muddy, derelict spot, imagining the old house seen through waving grasses and tall perennials. The large rectangular stone-walled enclosure at the front needed a certain sort of garden, one that linked it to the land around it. I didn't know then that I would actually live there.

The grazing is rough, tussocky and bumpy, and a mixture of open field and wood pasture. As the sides of the valley rise up, they become wooded or dotted with isolated trees. The river weaves along the bottom, seen from the map as a blue ribbon. A burn runs down alongside the house to join the East Allen. Boundaries are of dry-stone walls: mossy, lichened and with small gaps and cavities for wren or stoat. All these habitats meet at the house: field, walls, woodland, stand-alone trees, stream and river. The edges between vegetation zones are often species-rich, and it's this idea that I apply to the garden too.

We moved here in November 2009. The events that led up to it had been extremely difficult for me. For twenty-three years, I had been running a walled garden and nursery, Chesters Walled Garden, on Hadrian's Wall next to Chesters Roman Fort. It was a beautiful place, loved by many; four high brick walls sheltering a sunny two acres that sloped gently to the south. Having to leave, and worse still, needing to save the thousands of special plants, was a logistical nightmare. So many plants had histories, reminders of people and places, or had been collected over many years.

I carry with me every garden that I have had to leave. My childhood garden is still a place that I can walk through in my thoughts, influential on my thinking with its wild edges. Or the first tiny patch outside a rented farm cottage with its scrambling perennial sweet peas. A slightly bigger garden outside another rented cottage amongst upland fields. With them, I learnt and tried things out. Then came the two enclosed acres of Chesters that took nearly a quarter of a century to develop. Each was an increase in size, in confidence, in expression. Gardening has been a lifelong passion and it is what makes me who I am. And each garden has been so hard to leave.

Sometimes I return to Chesters in my dreams. The old key to the paint-peeled door hangs on my kitchen wall, its surface buffed and shiny from so many turns in the lock. I know what it feels like to open that door and step from the coolness of the woods into the reflected heat from the old bricks. To smell the resinous warmth emanating from the lean-to greenhouse, the musky tang of the box hedges. I can take myself along the paths, knowing exactly where I'm going, what weeds would always grow in certain spots, what jobs I'd have to do in each month of the year. I can still feel my way around that garden.

Having to leave was hard for others too. For my dear friend Tracy who ran the shop at weekends and left me funny little notes and who also returns to Chesters in her dreams. My children had gone there after school, hidden up a lilac tree, learnt how to take cuttings, played in the watering system and come running when they found a toad or a dragonfly. The herb borders were filled with plants gleaned with excitement from nurseries all over the country. The famous Thyme Bank was a collection filled with plants by my ex-husband, Kevin, his favourite area of the garden amongst the many parts he created. Over the years, the garden had taken me from shyness to being able to speak unscripted at lectures, to the many times we had filmed for television. I had grown with it. The loss of the garden affected us all and there was an outpouring of collective grief when it had to close.

To mark its passing, I started a memories book and people filled it with writings, drawings, photographs, poems and art. The painter Birtley Aris drew a beautiful frontispiece in his distinctive pen and ink style. Branches ferns and flowers arch over the words "Garden Memories of Chesters Walled Garden" and beneath that there is a quotation of Vita Sackville-West from *The Land*:

> *She walks among the loveliness she made,*
> *Between the apple-blossom and the water –*
> *She walks among the patterned pied brocade,*
> *Each flower her son, and every tree her daughter.*

Around the bottom edge of the page are flower-filled pots, a trug, part of a brick wall, a trowel and Birtley's signature 2010 in his beautiful flowing writing. There are happy memories on the pages: "We started coming to the garden when our children were small…each new visit was an adventure." A local artist wrote, "I heard black caps and watched long-tailed tits, disturbed slumbering toads and hidden moths." Another said, "As ever, this place has provided balm to the soul." Someone quoted from *The Song of Solomon*. Someone thanked me for the myrtle branches that I'd given her for her wedding. A friend began to heal after the death of her husband. The spirit in the book was one of celebration for what the garden had become but some could not hold back. "I was horrified to learn about the fate of Chesters Walled Garden. You must be so sad after a lifetime of love and work." The specialness of the place is evident in every person's contribution. I cannot read the book without filling up with emotion.

An exhibition was organised at the local arts centre, the Queen's Hall in Hexham. I had encouraged many artists over the years to use Chesters Walled Garden for inspiration and had often rounded a corner on a path to find someone sitting cross-legged by a pond, painting in a sketch book. I'd shown its herbs and abundant wildlife to schoolchildren, hoping to pass on the awareness of the natural world that I had known a child. *The Memories Book* was on display, the walls covered in artworks from people of all ages. The Queen's Hall funded a fold-out booklet, a collaboration of my writing and linocuts of flowers by artist and illustrator Kim Lewis. Four walls, twelve plants, each with memories and resonant with meaning. I wrote, "These are plants that I have especially loved, with stories stretching back into childhood or holding the thrill of a new discovery." It was entitled *Sanctuary*. It celebrated a walled garden, a paradise garden, a sanctuary from the world that would be a sanctuary no longer.

When word of the garden closing got out, it made the headlines of the local newspapers and was on the early evening news. So many people were affected by it that there were lots of offers of help. The November weather was not as kind, though, the soil sticky and clarty from rain, and I wrote in my diary, "What a terrible week to be attempting to move a garden." Towards the end of the month, a work party came to help; some were friends, others were generous people who I had never met. I had to direct what was going on right across the walled garden, my pockets stuffed with pens and labels, a notebook for recording lists of plants. I was continuously asked, "What next?" And I had to draw on my deep memory and intimate knowledge of this special place, to explain how a plant would divide, to be precise about what the roots would look like, what weeds to leave behind. By nightfall, I had a sore throat from talking so much and fell exhausted into bed.

Leaving a garden can be harder and more complicated than moving house. There were lists to make with a star rating to denote how important each item was. Digging up, bagging, triple labelling, root pruning trees, containerising, accepting help – none of the things that you could offload to a removal firm. Finding bulbs in autumn at a time when they were dormant meant relying on my knowledge of where they were, an intimacy with that garden that I had developed over so many years. My car smelt of earth and damp humus, with rustling bags of peonies to the roof of the boot and daffodils on the back seat. I wrote in my diary, "My car is such a mess! Each time I come home, I am laden with treasures that I don't want to leave behind." It felt like filling the ark. Except that these were plants, not animals that could go forth and multiply at their new land fall. All the plants that mattered most to me were re-established in our new garden. But here they would be freed from the constraints of an inherited garden layout and could express themselves.

The style of gardening that I had developed over the years of working the garden at Chesters was of burgeoning borders, spilling over with free-flowing plants. I'd learnt from it and developed as a gardener through the process. Starting again at our new house, where the garden had not been touched for years, was an opportunity, a blank canvas, weed-filled but ripe for making. It was a chance to liberate the planting, even from the fulsome and wide borders at Chesters. And it would suit the house and its position in its hidden valley.

A Garden in the Valley

It was not long after moving to Allendale that I began writing a *Country Diary* for *The Guardian*. The *Country Diary* has been *The Guardian*'s natural history column since 1906, and a collection was published for its 100-year anniversary. There was a rare get-together in London with all the diarists photographed including Veronica Heath, who was writing from Northumberland. I'd wanted to approach *The Guardian* for some ten years to see if I could contribute, but I never wanted to tread on the toes of Veronica, who I knew and liked. I finally wrote to the editor, coincidentally about the time that Veronica retired at eighty-three, though I didn't know that, and was asked to submit a couple of pieces of writing. I was told by the editor that she had put me on "a very long list". Somehow, I made it to the top of that list and wrote my first piece. I have now been contributing for thirteen years.

I had written diaries and nature notes for years, parallel to my life as a gardener, and suddenly it was all coming together. At a time when I had lost my job along with the end of the business that I had run for over half my working life, I was free to explore nature writing and to create a new garden. Chesters had been run organically and working with nature had been a priority. I could now link the two even more closely than before and explore ways of micro-imitating natural habitats within a garden setting in order to maximise the potential for wildlife.

Pausing at the sink as I wash my hands, a small movement outside the window catches my eye. A Jenny wren. This sprightly bird nips in and out of the base of the summerhouse, picking up insects that are too tiny for me to see from where I am standing. It slips, mouse-like, into a gap in the dry-stone wall, disappearing, then popping out again to work its way across the paving slabs. It's little incidents like these that bring joy to my day.

For many, a result of Covid has been a turning to and appreciation of the natural world. In these deeply unsettling times of pandemic, war and climate change, there's a constant background anxiety. Noticing nature on one's doorstep, the tiny events and small details, can be a great help. As I watch the wren, I think of nothing else, absorbed in its fast pace, its jerky tail, its quick, spirited life. The wren takes me into the moment, a pure time when nothing else exists except me and the bird.

This is what I get from nature and from gardening. It is mindfulness without effort. Not consciously trying to be mindful but aware with all my senses, connected to my body, sensations and emotions. I am absorbed in that moment. Observing nature is an opportunity for mindfulness, no matter how tiny the thing that is being observed. Or where. Walking along a pavement, there might be ivy-leaved toadflax trailing in loops along brickwork, the plant growing from a minute crevice. Perhaps the jak of jackdaws investigating a chimney pot or the scent of buddleia coming from waste ground, pulling in butterflies with its sweet nectar. These moments make me feel more alive because I am not thinking before or after, not thoughts of past or future.

My daily walk is a repetition, a tracing and retracing of the same ground, making me aware of the small changes that occur in our valley. Each day brings something new: the first chiffchaff, a dipper preening on a river stone, woodpeckers drumming to each other from different woods. Getting to know a small area, I look out for annual events such as the blooming of primroses on a cool north-facing bank. I scramble along its gradient to get a photograph on my phone for posting to social media. I climb down onto the riverbank for a coltsfoot flower to get close up to its perfect golden daisy. They are things from this small patch of Northumberland to share with others.

Small encounters with nature are reassuring, providing an awareness outside ourselves. A friend writes to me from her flat in Germany describing a wren on her balcony, lining its small nest first with bits of hedging and then with the moss. As I talk on the phone with another friend, I notice my first honeybee of spring on the window ledge, and a treecreeper skittering up the lichened bark of the ash tree. From others, I receive texts about skylarks on a farm, a red kite seen over Hexham, yellowhammers by the Tyne. We are all swapping observations of these little snippets of nature, encouraging and heartening.

I also share what I am doing in the garden by writing in magazines about the seasonal rhythms of producing vegetables and flowers. When I am working in the garden, I'm not really consciously thinking then either, yet something happens in the background. If I have a problem or something I am trying to resolve, I won't think about it directly or ruminate endlessly, as I might at three o'clock in the morning, but invariably I will leave the garden with a feeling of having sorted things out. It's a settling, a soothing, from hands in soil, weeding, pruning, creating pictures.

Many people turned towards gardening and nature during the pandemic. Sales of vegetable seeds rocketed, as did searches on websites for information on how to grow them. My son, when furloughed, made a small pond edged with bog plants so my grandchildren could see birds drinking, pond skaters and froglets. On their walks they'd look at dandelions, bracken fronds, birch bark and beetles. I have loved plants all my life. It's only now that I realise the significance of a story my parents used to tell – of how before I could talk properly I gazed in wonder at a daisy in the lawn and said "bibwee, bibwee". Ever after that they used the words to name something that was beautiful, simple and precious as "bibwee, bibwee". I couldn't live without plants. As someone said to me, my soul would shrivel up. My love of gardening and of the natural world has been passed on to my children and in turn to my grandchildren.

Second Nature

Looking back, I can trace the story of how I became a gardener and a naturalist. Being given my own small patch of garden, going on family walks, watching someone else cutting a hedge or digging the vegetable garden, noticing and drawing by copying the illustrations in bird books. Nature studies were included then in schoolwork. For the many who have no access to the outside and to green spaces, it is surely vital in creating awareness, to preventing that disconnect that is driving our ecological crisis. I was very unhappy at school, which was a Victorian strict place. But my favourite lesson was biology because the teacher took us on walks to a local pond, made us draw the way a seed splits and germinates or colourful fruiting fungi like the fairytale fly agaric. Of all the school notebooks, that biology one is the only one that I have kept.

I'd like to be able to tell that teacher what a difference she made to my life, along with others. The woman painter who gave me a box of watercolour pencils, lovely graded shades of colour lying in their pale blue cardboard box. My parents' elderly gardener who I followed round and who taught me the feel of gardening. The art teacher at school who gave us asparagus fern or lilies to draw, so that we looked and studied in order to understand how the plants were formed. A few years ago, on a visit to the Chelsea Flower Show, I chatted to garden designer Chris Beardshaw about the importance of children learning about the natural world and about encouraging them to be interested in growing. He said that when he was in his early teens, he was shown how to propagate plants by a nurseryman and that was what it took to fire his enthusiasm. "It just takes one person to flick the switch," he said.

The idea for this book came when I was giving a talk to Hexham Beekeepers in a village hall on a very wet Sunday in early October. The subject was Wildlife Gardening with especial emphasis on plants for pollinators. At the end, after some of the lengthiest clapping I've ever received, one man came up to me and said it had been "the best talk I've ever been to". What seemed to have really resonated with the audience were my descriptions of that particular richness that occurs at the crossing of habitats. That and the way that we can learn from it to create numerous small habitats in a garden. A friend, Clare Lindsay, came up to me saying, "I think I have the title for your next book – 'Where habitats meet'. It's what you said, they're your words, I'm just picking up on them." I instantly felt fired up and thought about it all the way home, a way of uniting garden and nature. I settled on a different title but it gave me my theme.

As a nature writer and gardener, I had long been wanting to write a book about gardening and a book about nature. Clare Lindsay inspired me to write about both since nature informs the way I garden and to show how I've worked to integrate the garden with the landscape. Living at the meeting of this patchwork of different habitats, I see the resulting diversity every day. In the way I garden, I aim to create lots of small habitats: layers, niches and places for each type of wildlife, starting with insects, which are the bridge between plants and animals and birds. I look at the richness that I see around me and learn from it to apply those ideas to the more intimate landscape of the garden. Wildlife flows across and through these artificial human boundaries providing there's as much to offer as there is outside. To the buzzard, mewing as it slowly circles high above, it's just another stone walled enclosure in this valley.

The Valley Landscape

On high ground and centrally placed between east and west coasts, the North Pennines National Landscape (previously AONB) is one of the most remote and unspoilt places in England. It's a landscape of moorland threaded through by dales and has 40 per cent of the UK's upland hay meadows. It's a place to see red squirrel, short-eared owl, black grouse and ring ouzel. A springtime walk is to the fluting, magical calls of curlew, golden plover and lapwing, wading birds come back to the moors to breed. The air resonates to the sound of drumming snipe, vibrating their tail feathers in a courtship display flight, and to the liquid trilling of larks rising above the grassy hills.

I am drawn to the uplands, to places where the soil is thin and the rocks are close to the surface like bones poking out of skin. Childhood holidays were mostly in Scotland, which was a complete contrast to Berkshire where I grew up. Part of the excitement was in getting there. We would drive to London to put the car on the sleeper train, traveling overnight up to Inverness. The neat and organised cabin had bunk beds with little netting pouches against the walls for stowing things, drop-down tables and a ladder to the top bunk. The train crossed the long curving Royal Border Bridge at Berwick, high above the River Tweed with its swans, and slowed into Edinburgh, where I would crane my neck to look up at the castle on its rock. Once the car was off the train, we would explore the Highlands, the heather always out because it would be August and the school holidays.

Perhaps I associate the wilder places with happier times and a release from school. Although I loved the softer landscape of the south with its water meadows, downland and chalk streams, it was – and is – in the hilly ground of sheep-cropped turf, of curlew, harebell and bent hawthorn that I feel most at home. The North Pennines has all this: heather moorland, fast-flowing upland rivers and stone-built villages snaking through the valleys. It's an area of international importance with its dark skies, its blanket bogs, rare arctic alpine plants and breeding waders. An amazing 36 per cent of the National Landscape is designated as Sites of Special Scientific Interest. England's biggest waterfall is High Force in Upper Teesdale where the River Tees plunges into the deep pool of a gorge.

It's in one of these North Pennine valleys that we live and garden. Allendale means "land of shining water". The River East Allen is fed by streams above the high village of Allenheads, a busy lead mining centre in the nineteenth century. All along the river are signs of the mining past, the most spectacular being a pair of chimneys on the peat lands above our little valley. A pair of flues, collapsed in places, run up the hillside and carried fumes from the lead smelt mill to the fell top, a distance of two miles. As lead and silver solidified on the inside of the arched stonework of the flues, they would be scraped off and recovered. Now all is quiet. It was from this heathery high point that I wrote my first *Country Diary* for *The Guardian* in 2011, and a place that I return to often for its far views to the Cheviots, for the sight of the northern lights in frosty winter. It's up here in May that I set a pheromone lure to attract emperor moths, *Saturnia pavonia*, strikingly marked in silver and charcoal (the females), or burnt orange and umber (the males), with four large spots, dark as owls' eyes. The lure mimics the female's scent and it only takes a short time before several males arrive, full of restless energy, bumping into my hair, twirling in the air, dancing around the lure. Up here too I find violet oil beetles, *Meloe violaceus*, iridescent and aubergine-coloured, common lizards on warm days, and have thrilling views of short-eared owls, *Asio flammeus*, mottled brown with staring yellow eyes.

This is only two miles from our house but it couldn't be more different. Up at the chimneys, the heather stretches away, unbroken by trees or features, a single habitat of peaty moorland. Down in the valley, it's a mixture of habitats and visual contrasts from field, woods and river. There's a temperature difference too, with often a drop of two degrees from the upper side of the valley to our garden. If the general Allendale forecast is for −4° I know it is likely to be −6° at our house. Hard winters can seem like permafrost.

Walk into the valley from either end and it gently opens out. There's only room for one wide level field between its sloping sides. Where the river has moved across it over time are the terraced signs of earlier banks. There are copses, home to roe deer and buzzard, and fragments of semi-ancient woodland. A medley of trees: larch, Scots pine, oak, birch and willow. To the west is a hay meadow studded with orchids and wood cranesbill. Something about the way the valley is concealed from outside view makes the place settle on you like a cloak.

The map's blue ribbon of the East Allen threads along the valley bottom. On one side is the sheltering curve of a steep wood, its south-facing slope of oak, sycamore and bird cherry under-carpeted in dog's mercury, wild garlic, wood anemone and early purple orchid. Light filters through the canopy onto fallen ivy-covered trees and in spring, primroses gleam out of the depths. Outgrown hazel coppice attracts squirrels in autumn.

The woods on the other side are more open, with beeches topping little knolls, curiously like parkland, where the deer like to lie up, as if there's truth in the story I was told of nineteenth-century planned planting. It's rough pasture on the hillside slopes and in the valley bottom, unfertilised and grazed by a rotation of sheep and cattle. Moorhens slip in and out of the thickets of willow that fringe a small pond, a favourite place too for heron and some-times as many as thirty mallards. Frogspawn forms jellied lumps amongst the rushes of the pond outlet. Barn owls quarter the long grasses on the hunt for voles.

The wet places in the valley bottom form their own special hab-itat, that of wood pasture. Here grow the alders, some of which are many years old. Wood pasture is a unique habitat that evolved from a balance between farming and trees grown for wood. These veteran trees are multi-trunked, leading me to wonder if perhaps they were coppiced by lead miners since alder wood has been used to make charcoal and gunpowder. Years of being nibbled by sheep have fashioned the base of their trunks into calloused growths, the lumps and bumps of their rough bark looking like accretions of candle wax. I have often photographed and drawn these char-acterful trees, filling my sketchpad with details of catkins, cones, patterns of bark, growths of burr and the lichens and mosses that live on them. Kestrels use the tree tops as perches. Bats nest in dark holes and slime moulds, resembling gobbets of marshmal-low, shine white against rotten wood. Marsh marigolds, *Caltha palustris*, flourish in the wet soil beneath their light shade, deep golden cups opening to the early spring sunshine. Their branches are a shelter for the sheep in the heat of summer and it is that equilibrium between grazing and trees that gives wood pasture its beauty and distinctiveness.

Records show that our house has been here since at least 1661, standing at the junction between the burn and the East Allen. Or at least a house has stood on this spot and been rebuilt over the years. The large quoins around the door and the depth of the walls suggest it maybe dates from the end of the bastle building period, that time in Northumberland's turbulent past when stone houses were made to a defensive design. Allendale is scattered with bastles, some in ruins such as nearby Rowantree

Stob, some still lived in. Fortified farmhouses, the word is said to come from the French for castle, "*bastille*". They were necessary even after the Union of Scotland and England in 1603 since reiving (raiding to plunder cattle and goods) carried on into the seventeenth century. Strong rectangular buildings, bastles have walls a metre thick. Animals could be housed in the ground floor especially during a raid, and the family lived above. The upper level could only reached by a ladder, which would be hauled up at night. Sometimes bastles were grouped together for defence as at Monk, a farm that lies a few miles to the west of our valley. The walls of our house are not wide enough to suggest that it might have been a bastle, but their depth allows for window seats from where we can look out over the garden. With its stone roof, our house feels part of the landscape. It feels like an intersection, a meeting place between water and stone, field and wood, canopy and openness, light and dark.

None of this I thought about consciously when we were looking for somewhere to live and to start again. I was instinctively drawn to the land and to its special mix of qualities. It was quite simply the right place to make a garden. Having spent nearly a quarter of a century nurturing and refining the garden at Chesters, it would take an extraordinary place to match it for atmosphere. It made the leaving of the walled garden easier to bear. On 12th April 2010, I went back to Chesters for the last time and to fill my car with a few last-minute plants. These included three different sages – a favourite being an old pink-flowered sage – that I had left as long as possible because of the cold weather. It was a bright spring morning and the garden looked tidy, all the paths neatly raked and the borders tended, but with an empty feeling. One or two early butterflies were on the wing, a chiffchaff was calling and there were a few bumblebees. I met with the estate secretary and we walked the garden together, a final round. She said how hard it must be to leave after all these years. I told her I would particularly miss the wildlife and the wonderful soil. It was a dignified calm exit as I handed over the key to the garden door. As I drove away, a woman was rootling around in the skip in the car park, salvaging wonky yew trees, tattered herbs and even an old peeling paint sign from the Thyme Bank. I felt a sense of relief as well as loss, but also a freedom as I drove south to home and a new garden to be made.

Starting with the Soil

It can be scary as well as exciting to begin a new garden. The process of moving house is as stressful as they say and we felt shell-shocked that first morning and unsure if we had done the right thing. We'd left the security of a village home for the unknown, for a potholed track and a river that might rise in flood and which just a week later gave us our first experience of what it was like in spate. We questioned our decision and it wasn't helped by someone who said to me, "We all think you're mad to move there." Another said, "We think you are very brave." Oh dear.

There was no garden here when we moved to Allendale. Long grass sprouted between the paving stones of the terrace and there was rubbish everywhere. Amongst the tall growth of docks, nettles and creeping thistle were weedkiller containers, a broken bird table, the twisted metal of a polytunnel, half-burnt tree stumps, coils of barbed wire, plywood, oil drums and the rumpled plastic sheeting of a large swimming pool. By the gate was a huge heap of rubble and soil that had to be cleared, under which we discovered three old motorbike engines. Ten butler's sinks lay in the field, their enamel pitted and scarred, a job lot from eBay. Decomposing straw bales slumped at angles amongst rosebay willowherb, brambles and tree saplings. Where retaining walls had collapsed, the fallen stones had broken the paving slabs.

The previous owner had levelled the ground, scooping up much of the precious topsoil to dump it over the boundary wall on the riverbank. A fuzz of green was starting to grow amongst the chevron tread marks of dumper truck and bulldozer and the rocks that were scattered across the surface. Hawthorn branches swept to the ground, impenetrably spiny, hiding plastic bottles, soggy cardboard boxes and rusting metal. Clearing it all away took many trips to the local tip, the swimming pool alone, cut into manageable pieces, filling three trailer loads. Clearing the paved terraces liberated the sandstone slabs from the grass and weeds that had made them look so abandoned. The gradual cutting back of dead stems, foliage and branches revealed a satisfyingly rectangular garden space.

I knew that the alluvial soil should be good for growing but it was only as I did some exploratory digging that I could feel it between my fingers. It had a pleasing quality, crumbly and slightly sandy yet retentive, but what shocked me was the complete lack of worms. The soil seemed deadened, crushed by heavy machinery, compacted and empty of invertebrates and life. The first thing we needed to do was to get organic matter back into the land, to build compost bins and incorporate anything we could get our hands on: spent hops, grass clippings, manure, leafmould and leafy weeds. It was therefore rather ironic that the first job involved more machinery in the form of a digger.

The front garden, lined by dozer tracks, had had its mass of nettles and rocks buried during the ground levelling. We brought with us a mass of plants dug up from Chesters in several horse box loads – imagine how many plants I wanted to rescue from a two-acre walled garden – and were pressed for time to get them into new ground. It would take many months to dig the new garden by hand so we asked for ploughing help from a local contractor. He came up with an inventive solution, to use a digger to lift out the stones and thick mats of nettle roots, and loosen the soil using the slotted bucket on the digger as a giant riddle. His driver, Peter Armstrong, he said, did "a very tidy job" and could be paid by the hour, working in stages to allow us to catch up with the finer stone picking. A job that had seemed overwhelming now seemed feasible and freed me up for writing.

Starting with the Soil

In the last summer at Chesters Walled Garden, I had had a chance meeting with Tamsin Westhorpe, then editor of *The English Garden* magazine. After saying how much she admired the atmosphere and planting style of the garden, she was saddened to hear that I would have to leave it all behind. It gave her the idea for an article on what it is to leave a garden, something most gardeners have to face at some point through moving house, illness or, in my case, the ending of a lease. She imagined it as a celebration of the twenty-three years spent creating the garden as well as a valediction. It was published under the heading *The Long Goodbye* and illustrated with the beautiful photographs of Andrea Jones. I admired Tamsin's spontaneity and her ability to think of an idea and suggest it there and then when so many editors would have mulled it over and emailed later. It's what makes the voice of her garden articles – and her book *Diary of a Modern Country Gardener* – so direct and accessible.

The article, one that I wrote from the heart, then led to another idea of hers, that I should write a monthly column on the making of the new garden. This would run for two years, an unusual length of time for a gardening magazine, under the title of *A Garden Reborn*, with each month coming out the year after it had happened. This became the motivation for making progress and a challenge through two snowbound winters. That first year, just one month into writing the series, we were snowed in for two weeks. Everything stops for snow – no walling, no gardening, no sorting things out – but somehow I needed to find material to write about, so wrapping up newly moved plants, planning the layout, coppicing hazel for garden structures all happened quite naturally.

Winter in the North Pennines is breathtakingly lovely, totally silent, each tree or branch outlined in white, field walls encrusted as if candle wax has flowed down their sides, animal tracks visible, the river darker than the land, the sky alternatively wan and grim or flushed with pink. I wondered how my plants were coping under their frozen blanket. The temperature dropped to -13 and we struggled to keep warm in the house with few seasoned logs left and no deliveries able to get through. We still had to sort out the heating and had to warm the bedroom from a tiny Victorian fireplace. Ourselves and our cat huddled by the black painted hearth.

David skied to the village for supplies, managing to fill a rucksack with milk and eggs without breaking them. When the snow finally shifted, it left a messy brown landscape patched with straggling areas of white. There was dirt and debris everywhere and ice solidified still on our track. Yet when it melted, I found a Mexican daisy still alive in a pot having survived -16. Snow is a great insulator, though it was still surprising for this rather tender South American plant.

It was now the end of January and we had been waiting since mid-November for Peter Armstrong to be able to start work. He had only done one afternoon before the ground became too frozen and the digger had frustratingly stood idle in front of the house all that time. For two days a week for over a month, I found it hard to concentrate on writing magazine articles because of the racket going on outside the window. Peter would make scoops into the ground with the large metal bucket, shaking it violently and noisily, before dropping the stones in a large pile. A pattern became revealed in lines of riddled soil as he worked backwards from the eastern boundary wall beneath the sycamores before beginning again at the wall. The ratio was staggering, almost 50 per cent was rocks, but the soil left behind was lovely, rich and dark and felt good to handle. It took a chunk out of my minimal garden budget, but with every bucket I thought of what it saved us doing by hand. The rocks would all be useful in laying the foundations of the paths.

Peter's dog, a black Labrador called Jay, usually sat alongside side him in the cab but wasn't able to because of the vibration and noise. Instead he lay on the drive, waiting until break time when he could be with Peter again. He was only allowed in the digger as Peter moved from one part of the garden to start on the next. Then Jay sat there looking out over the glass front with a blissed-out expression on his face.

Although there was very little life in this front garden soil, there was even less in the land behind the house. In all my gardening career, I had never known soil that had no worms in it at all. This area had to be dug entirely by hand in arm-jarring repetitions of fork and spade. The amount of stones was staggering. David photographed me with the large pile of rubble I had extracted from making just one small border.

The priority that first spring was to revitalise the soil, and to begin with compost making. David made three linked wooden compost bins in a sunny position next to the beginnings of a vegetable garden – fourteen rows of potatoes that we would give to friends and family as well as store for ourselves but planted principally to break up the soil. He sunk eight square wooden posts directly onto the earth, boxed in by metre-long boards on three sides with moveable slats on the fronts. He used a spirit level to get the horizontals and verticals. Fourteen years on they have produced several cubic metres of compost every year, all laid on top of the vegetable garden for worms to take down into the soil using no-dig methods.

And worms came. We made that first fill of the compost bin using soft, fleshy weeds (no roots), the old straw bales that had been lying around, spent hops from the brewery a mile away, torn cardboard, kitchen waste and lawn clippings. It was immensely satisfying to begin composting and to return everything back to the garden. David made neat compost duvets to create warmth:

layers of bubble wrap between the black plastic of inside-out sacks. He turned it from one bin to the next every ten days or so and very soon the earthy-smelling rotting mass contained fruit fly maggots, centipedes, millipedes, woodlice – and pink brandling worms.

In my childhood garden, there were no sacks of compost to be bought from garden centres to use in the greenhouse. Seedlings and bedding plants were raised in old tomato boxes lined with newspaper, a layer of leafmould and then sieved compost and soil. The boxes were made of very thin wood and had colourful pictures of plump red tomatoes against blue skies. They disintegrated after a few seasons, the bottom slats rotting through watering, layers of damp newspaper sticking to the wood. Annual bedding plants and vegetable seedlings would need separating out, unlike today's plug trays. The sieved soil became rounded into little balls like the topping for apple crumble.

Leafmould for the trays of seedlings came from a large richly dark heap, many years old, encased in bent chicken wire. Into it went the annual harvest of all the leaves from the many trees around the house, leaves that had collected on lawns, paths and driveway. Best of all for a child, it held the palmate leaves and conkers from five large horse chestnut trees, and in spring I'd see how a creamy root could force its pale way out of a shiny caramel-coloured conker to delve down into the layers of leafmould. I was fascinated by the emerging shoots, curving upwards, the hand-like folded leaves opening to five-pointed symmetry. I transplanted some of these into an area of rough grass, hoping they wouldn't get cut down by mistake when it was scythed in August.

Perhaps my fascination with composting came from my father's father. A friend of the botanist Sir Albert Howard, my grandfather was a founder member of the Soil Association. My dad used to talk about the Indore Method of composting, which, as a child,

I thought meant it was made indoors. In the 1920s, Howard ran a research farm at Indore, the capital of Madhya Pradesh in central India, and wrote in his small but influential book, *The Waste Products of Agriculture*, about a year-round process of making compost in shallow pits. His work made him a principal figure of the early organic farming movement.

I was fascinated too by the grass snakes (*Natrix natrix*) that bred in the warmth and constant temperature of the compost heap. Here they could incubate their eggs, safe from predators, and I remember the thrill of finding a writhing mass of hatchling snakes amongst decomposing lawn clippings. A beautiful female grass snake will lay between ten and forty white leathery eggs in June or July, incubating them until they hatch in early autumn. This means they shouldn't be disturbed and the compost shouldn't be turned if it's likely that they are present.

Grass snakes are at the northern edge of their range in the North Pennines so I've never seen one in our valley. Up on the moors there are adders *(Vipera berus)* but in our garden it is slow worms *(Anguis fragilis)* that live in the compost and the occasional common lizard *(Zootoca vivipara)* in the retaining walls. When I first came to Northumberland in the 1970s, I quite often saw adders. Out exploring heather moorland and the quiet uplands, I'd find them basking on slabs of rock or dry turf mounds, absorbing sunlight. Their dark zigzag markings on a grey or reddish-brown background resemble fabric patterns. Sometimes I would see several in an afternoon, and one even curled up on the warm material of my rucksack as I sat eating a sandwich. There has been a noticeable decline in numbers since then, and I can now go a year without seeing an adder at all.

Although the adder is Britain's only venomous snake, it is very rare to get bitten and then only in defence because it has been disturbed or accidentally trodden upon. An adder is much more likely to disappear into cover. When David was fell running on the moors above Allendale, he leapt a small burn and landed inches from an adder, luckily not hurting himself or the snake. I do know someone who was bitten by an adder when planting trees, though he didn't realise it at the time. Feeling like he had flu by evening, he noticed a couple of small puncture wounds above his ankle. Unaware that he had been bitten at the time meant that he kept calm, which helped prevent the spread of venom through his body.

Adders are able to swim, though it's something that is rarely observed. Once after heavy rain of the kind that gets set in on the North Pennine fell tops, the track I was walking at the RSPB's Geltsdale Nature Reserve had collected wide spreads of puddles. An adder, startled by footsteps, launched itself across the water, head held just above the surface, propelling itself along by muscular S-shaped movements.

It is slow worms that we are therefore most likely to see in our garden, in particular around or in the moist, warm conditions of the compost heaps. I will be head-down gardening when I hear David call out that he has seen one and I rush over to enjoy the moment. We have laid a rectangle of rusty corrugated iron on the soil near the compost heaps so that it can be lifted to see if there is a slow worm underneath it, warmed by the sun on metal. They come out generally at dusk to search for worms, spiders, insects and slugs, making them helpful to gardeners. Slow worms are not snakes but legless lizards, sleek and shiny, with eyelids and a flat, forked tongue. They are drawn to the compost by the heat and the plentiful worms and slugs.

In summer, I might find the remains of an egg sac. Unlike snakes, slow worms' eggs are laid internally and they give birth to live young, which can hatch as they are laid or shortly afterwards. There can be litters of six to twelve baby slow worms, which are immediately independent, living up to twenty years, possibly more. If attacked, a slow worm's defence mechanism is to shed its tail, which writhes on the ground, distracting the predator and enabling an escape. This is what gives rise to its specific name of "*fragilis*". In winter, they hibernate under a rotting log or under-ground, another reason for leaving areas of the garden that are undisturbed.

The wide meadow verge that fringes the lawn gives safe passage to small mammals and to slow worms. Using the traditional hay time of early August to cut it, I do this with shears on my hands and knees rather than a strimmer, which might do injury to creatures such as slow worms. Clipping the meadow's edge by a stone wall, I encountered a large slow worm, grateful that I was working slowly and using one-handed sheep shears.

By the time the compost has cooled and is ready to be spread on the soil, the slow worms will have left. Of the three bins there is always one that is being added to with new material, one that has been turned and one that is ready for use. Lifting the front's wooden slats, David forks it into a wheelbarrow to line the trench for potatoes or beans, or to lay across the vegetable beds as a mulch. Through repeated turning, it has heated enough to kill off any seeds, which makes for less weeding. It was in the box-edged vegetable beds at Chesters Walled Garden that we began adopting no-dig gardening, inspired by the work of Charles Dowding. Charles has written numerous books and his website is generously detailed, showing comparison photographs between dig and no-dig and the results of the many tests that he has carried out.

Charles began growing vegetables in the early 1980s and very quickly created a market garden based on no-dig principles and inspired by three pioneer gardeners: Arthur Guest, F.C. King and Shewell Cooper. Having visited plenty of organic gardens, he felt that their chaotic weed growth got in the way of producing abundant crops so controlling weeds became his priority. He used straw on the paths and worked at building up good soil structure on the un-trampled beds with mulches of compost. Since those days, and several gardens in between, he now runs the exemplary Homeacres in Somerset and enthusiastically shares his knowledge via courses, books and television.

In no-dig systems, the soil is undisturbed, and layers of organic matter provide it with life, all drawn down by worms that aerate the soil and provide drainage. It is much like the natural processes that occur in nature, in particular woodland with yearly deposits of fallen leaves. When we began making our garden, it was full of creeping thistles from the fields, but layers of thick cardboard that were then covered in mulch eradicated these within a year or two. The only problem that we discovered after a few years was the effect of the network of roots from trees quite a distance away. Charles advised digging a trench on the side of the vegetable beds to interrupt the roots and this has worked pretty well.

Our growing season may be shorter than some other parts of the country but the garden is still highly productive. Garlic planted in November and lifted to be dried in July provides a year-round supply. Onions and shallots, leeks and chives add to the crop of alliums and do well in the light alluvial soil and with no competition from weeds. Lettuces and other salads, begun as plugs in the greenhouse, are planted out under cloches in early spring with broad beans and peas being direct sowed, supported by the pruning of hardy fuchsias and other twigs. By summer and strawberry time, a wooden trug from the garden will be a colourful cornucopia of ripened fruit, courgettes, beans, parsley, herbs and bright orange calendula flowers. Potatoes and beet-roots, purple French beans, cherry red tomatoes and cucumbers from the greenhouse; we revel in the fullness and abundance of our allotment-sized patch.

Starting with the Soil

It's all very different from the original weed-filled stagnant soil where there were no worms. Now song thrushes and blackbirds find plenty of food for their chicks, dunnocks and wrens forage in the leafiness and bumblebees feed in the pale trumpets of bean flowers. Hazel poles from the nearby wood support runner beans way above head and, like the Flower Garden, the growth is in tiers and layers to satisfy the needs of a wide range of wildlife. When I need a bit of calm it is to the Veg Garden that I go, with its neat lines and its feeling of vitality and purpose.

Anchored Wildness:
the Garden's Design

The advice on making a garden is often to live with it for a while, to get a feel for the place and to see what is already growing there. It was late October when we moved house and the ground needed to be ready to receive the plants from Chesters within a few months. There was no time to draw a design or to make a planting plan. I had to rely completely on instinct, on confidence and on the accumulated thoughts of a lifetime's gardening. It was liberating and exciting.

In my garden diary, there's a scribbled idea for the front Flower Garden. Just four paths divide the 45 by 25 metre space that is set within the stone-walled boundary. When I roughed out the idea, we had just dug up four topiary yews from Chesters, plants that I had originally found as seedlings in the borders and had brought on. There were yew trees growing in the surrounding woods but just outside the walled garden was a tree that had been dated to 700 years old. I like to think that the seedlings might have come from this ancient tree. The four yews were different shapes but I noted in my diary, "I've an instant inspiration that they should form the centre crossing of two paths making it a pivotal point."

My simple plan was this: a path directly in line with the front door with the longer cross path set back by two thirds, ideally a greenhouse at the end of the cross path, and a fourth path to edge a woodland border beneath the line of sycamores on the west. It would be asymmetrical to echo the pleasing asymmetry of the house, which is longer to one side of the front door than the other. This would create four large and uninterrupted flowing borders, an expansion of the kind of meadow-like plant associations I had experimented with at Chesters, all on a much larger scale. The yews were the catalyst for the design.

In the end, because of that snowy winter, they were left bare-rooted on the terrace, swaddled in straw and bubble wrap through freezing temperatures for three months and somehow survived. Fourteen years on, they have matured and I have clipped them all to the same domed shape, their smooth curves contrasting in summer with exuberant perennials, their winter shapes under snow like plum puddings smothered in white sauce. I clip them using long handled topiary shears, enjoying the whole body movement that sharpens the sweep of their flanks. The yew domes are the central pivot. They create stability that anchors the planting and allows it to flow around them.

That late winter, having just moved to the new house, we were still digging up the plants from Chesters helped by friends and volunteers. Tutors and students came from the horticulture course at Newcastle College where I let them help themselves to anything from the sales area and surplus plants from the garden. Overhearing me talking about having to leave the garden tidy, they offered to strim and rake the borders. So many people lent a hand and I was touched by the loyalty and support for a garden that had meant so much to others too. Local nurseries took away stock plants, pots from the nursery were offered on Freecycle and the car park was full. The publicity that the garden's closure received in the press resulted in lots of volunteers and I was able to give them divisions too; the plants from Chesters took on a new life, scattered throughout Northumberland gardens.

In March, the digger had worked through part of the Flower Garden and we had gone over the soil, stone picking and weeding. As fast as I could, I got bare-rooted perennials into the new ground with no time for detailed planning but just feeling what would make good combinations. A six-foot-tall corkscrew hazel was dug up and moved to our new garden within the day, filling a trailer. There were little red female flowers on its mad twisted branches as well as dangling catkins. I got a thrill from seeing a robin alight on the hazel within one hour of it being put in position – the first shrub in what had been derelict, lifeless ground.

The garden needed a thoughtful aesthetic in response to its setting. I wanted it to connect with the landscape of field and hill and not impose itself. There would be no hedge within the stone walled boundary and very few shrubs so that the perennial meadow-like planting would rise and fall through the year. I want to feel the seasons progress and change, to see the contrast between February when very little is visible and October when seedheads rise above my head. That movement makes it feels alive. The garden would be like an exploded meadow, echoing the hay meadows of the North Pennines but on a much taller scale.

Each year I curate and make changes to that original planting, deciding which self-seeders to leave and which to take out, discarding ideas that haven't worked and moving in new plants. Or perhaps I am like the conductor of an orchestra, sometimes moving my baton gently through the air, at other times vigorously. I've learnt to be tough. Essentially, though, it is the same as when first planted. There are two guiding principles: one to do with the seasonal flow and the other to do with colour. The garden acts as a calendar, charting the year as one wave of planting takes over from another. It begins in the woodland border to the west, where late winter and early spring treasures flower beneath the sycamores before the canopy casts shade. Winter aconites are first to bloom, then snowdrops and snowflakes, lungworts, hellebores and epimediums until foliage and flowers fill the space, covering bare soil and leafmould. It becomes an unstoppable flow as, with April and May, the borders rise up once more, and aquilegias, alexanders and honesty join in, spilling across the huge borders moving ever eastwards. Summer erupts with peonies, alliums and geraniums as the borders gain height, culminating in a crescendo of acteas, cardoons and grasses far taller than me.

The second principle, used to create an increased sense of depth from our windows, is to have hot colours nearest the house with cooler colours further away. Based on art theory, it's an optical illusion where cool colours recede whilst warm colours seem to advance, increasing perception of depth. Keeping these two concepts in mind made it easier for me to work fast in that first and very dry spring with horsebox loads of bare-rooted plants from Chesters needing to be put in the soil as soon as possible. I would look at a plant and decide where it would fit, with little themes developing – to one side, purple leaves and flowers because I had seen how lovely the evening light is coming through their stained glass window petals. I had recently been to a talk about the Glasgow School and thoughts of Goethe's colour theory added another layer; the dynamism of complimentary colours near the house with those closer to each other in the colour wheel towards the back to add further distance. So amongst the hot yellows, oranges and reds I would toss in green or blue with *Geranium* 'Rozanne' mixed with helenium and cosmos, then a soft haze of whites and pale pinks towards the back wall.

The idea of the calendar is influenced by the garden of Herterton House, one of my favourites places and one that I have visited for more than thirty years. Designed by Frank and Marjorie Lawley, it is a garden that draws on the work of twentieth-century colour theorists such as Klee and Mondrian, as well as the oriental carpets that Frank collected and the use of herbs in old Northumbrian gardens. Five gardens surround the seventeenth-century house: a topiary garden presenting an organised public face towards the road, a physic garden in the old granary yard, a fancy garden of box parterres, a nursery garden and the crowning glory, which is the Flower Garden. This is influenced by the compositions of Mondrian and his division of space by black lines into varying sizes of squares and rectangles. A strong design underpins this surprising and exciting area filled with unusual plants. Instead of flower borders that are viewed from one side, the right-angled paths lead in and through the colour-themed planting.

Herterton's Flower Garden with its topiary, its waist hedges, its stone bowls and neat paths works as a sensual experience, but there is an extra and subtle layer of meaning to the colours in this garden: they represent the passage of time throughout the day. This symbolism ebbs out from the building, colours flowing out across the garden space. Nearest the house are the delicate yellows, pinks, creams and whites of dawn. Blocks of colour gather in intensity until the beds are vibrant with orange and blue, reminiscent of the sun at its zenith in a cloudless sky. Lastly come the violent colours of sunset, reds, blacks and deep purples, with cooler blues and silvers to either side. It is as if a painting had been laid out upon the ground, translated into three dimensions but constantly evolving with the seasons. Frank has written about the story of its making over the past forty-five years in *Herterton House and A New Country Garden*, and with Herterton having an uncertain future it is a valuable record of this admired and important late twentieth-century garden.

In the early days, the Lawleys made trips down to see the late Marjorie Fish at her garden at East Lambrook Manor in Somerset, driving back up north with a car stuffed full of rare plants swaddled in moss. They searched in the farm and cottage gardens of Northumberland for old varieties that were no longer commercially available. I in turn bought plants from the Lawleys, bagged up in damp newspaper; no plastic pots were ever used in their small nursery. Some of their perennials are now in our garden but something that's not much used at Herterton are grasses, perhaps because they tone down and subtract from the expanse of colour. I use grasses threaded through the borders as a way of connecting visually to the hillside, when in late summer and autumn they becoming increasingly straw coloured, wild and waving.

This linking of inside and out, of the world within the stone-walls and the landscape beyond, was a part of the plan right from the beginning. In the farthest corner from the house is an exuberant pampas grass, *Cortaderia richardii*, a finer, more delicately plumed species than the clump-headed types. Rather than being in isolation in a lawn, as it is so often grown, it forms the natural apex of the border before seeing the hill beyond. In front of it is a sweep of pink meadowsweet, *Filipendula rubra 'Venusta'*, a candyfloss mass of fluffy flowerheads and a reference to the wild and scented creamy meadowsweet that grows in the valley. In this corner too I grow angelica, *Angelica archangelica*, so that the green globes of flowers pick up on the shapes of the trees up on the hill. This in one of the very best plants for insects, much loved by hoverflies and providing nectar and pollen for bees. When I walk past it at the height of its nectar flow, the air is suddenly filled with insects lifting off from its green flowers.

Another element that links to the surrounding landscape is an elderly viburnum. When we came here, there were only four plants in the whole garden: a pear tree, a cherry and two overgrown viburnums. I found that this ragged, wild-looking shrub was a nest site for several species of birds; blackbird, dunnock, wren and robin all living together within its dense network of branches. With the nesting season over, I fashioned it into rounded shapes so that it now echoes the skyline sycamore, an association that I appreciate when I sit on the back terrace looking outwards.

Outside the garden walls, the fields are of rough grazing, with great drifts of creeping thistle that fill the air with sweetness when they flower. Insects and particularly butterflies cluster in their purple tops, with painted ladies if it is one of their years of mass migration. The thistles release snowstorms of downy seeds in late summer, and I hope for a westerly wind to take them away from the garden. Goldfinches cluster on the seedheads, large undulating flocks taking off as I walk past. Within the garden walls I echo the thistles in tall stands of red-purple *Cirsium rivulare* 'Atropurpureum' and purple pink *Cirsium tuberosum*. The former is now a staple with designers of gardens at the Chelsea Flower Show, the latter is a rare UK native, a perennial with long grey-green serrated leaves. Although it stays in a neat clump, it will self-seed, the opposite of melancholy thistle, *Cirsium heterophyllum*, which doesn't seed in my garden but spreads vigorously by creeping runners.

This beautiful wildflower likes the cool northern uplands and was once a common meadow plant of the North Pennines. The purple-red thistles grow on stout stems, some with branched flowerheads, some solitary. Any spines are soft and not prickly, the large leaves felted and pale underneath. It was once used to treat melancholia or depression, presumably due to the Doctrine of Signatures, the indication coming from the single and sometimes initially drooping flowerheads. In his *Complete Herbal* of 1653, Nicholas Culpeper writes, "…the decoction of the thistle in wine being drank, expels superfluous melancholy out of the body, and makes a man as merry as a cricket". Due to farming practices, melancholy thistle has retreated to track-sides and road verges, places where chemical sprays have not reached, where it forms uplifting banks of purple. Growing these thistles, along with strong forms such as cardoon and globe artichoke, creates a visual link between the outside and inside of the boundary walls.

All this happened without planning as I had to make instant decisions as to where plants should go. With volunteers asking me where to position each new arrival, I had to go entirely on feel as to whether or not it was in the right place. It might be based on light or shade, but mainly how it would work in combination with others in groups of plants, in small communities that were developing. It was an exciting process as I revelled in the spontaneity and in the feeling of freedom.

Key to allowing such freedom of planting was having some elements of stability. The box-edged parterre beds at Chesters had been filled with blocks of herbaceous colour: two rectangles entirely filled with tall purple *Verbena bonariensis* book-ending two squares of *Salvia nemorosa* and two squares of sedums, these four with the inside corners cut off. At the centre was a circle of lady's mantle, *Alchemilla mollis*, its lime green flowers frothing around an old sundial. As you looked across the parterre, the purple-blue of the salvia against the yellow-green of the lady's mantle was uplifting and dynamic.

Having dug up many sacks full of the sedums, now correctly called *Hylotelephium spectabile*, I wondered how to use them in my new design. They had to be included for their abundant insect life, but I did not feel their rounded shapes would fit with the loose, meadow-like forms of the new borders. I decided to make them into an edging down the central path in line with the front door, to create an autumn feast for bees and butterflies. In order to exaggerate the perspective and to increase the sense of depth when looking out from the house, the line along which they were planted drew in slightly in the distance.

These sedums have been an absolute joy. They have given definition to the Flower Garden and delighted with the various stages of growth, foliage and flowers that they go through. Even in winter, their rich brown tones contrast with the dark green of the yew domes and the freshness of frost and snow. Between the sedums and the path, I planted groups of the drumstick allium, *Allium spaerocephalum*, striking maroon egg-shaped flowers whose seedheads lean gracefully in the autumn winds and persist into winter. Against the back wall and looking back at the house is a pretty bench, on either side of which are a pair of amelanchiers, small shrubs with delicate-looking white flowers that nonetheless stand up to early spring winds. Their leaves turn orange-red in autumn, their small black berries eaten by blackbirds and thrushes. We prune the multi-stemmed specimens to create openness and so that the pattern of trunks holds winter interest.

With the double lines of sedums stretching away from the house, the cross path called for something similar in terms of singleness of purpose. So it naturally fell into place that the peonies would run all the way down on either side and lead to where we planned to have a greenhouse. Having brought with me a wide selection of peony cultivars, whole sacks filled with their bulbous, promise-rich tubers, it seemed right to group them together in this way. Single flowers with white petals and golden stamens, frou-frou pinks, vivid carmines and double blood-reds, they were a mix of scented varieties, of cottage garden types and the species *Paeonia officinalis* of herbalism. The myth about peonies not flowering after they have been moved is probably due to incorrect planting depth. Luckily, being March, it was a good time of year to move them, and we replanted with the eye buds just below the soil surface. Plant too deep and they can fail to flower or take years to do so. I noted in my diary that one clump had three flower spikes the first year, seven the second and twenty-nine the third.

Interspersed with the peonies, I used the front of the border for a geranium that was new to me, a gift from geranium expert Robin Moss, and one of the most impressive flowers of this useful group of plants. With huge white single flowers and pinkish red veins, *Geranium* 'Derrick Cook' is named for the man who collected it in Nepal in 1985. It spreads gently by runners so is easy to propagate and, having begun with three plants, I was able to divide it many times so it could be used at intervals all the way down the path. Other plants form regular and balanced shapes on the cross path: the large catmint, *Nepeta* 'Six Hills Giant', that spills over and disguises the edging boards, the brilliant red tulip 'Apeldoorn', which naturalises well, and the large-flowered *Allium christophii*. Its enormous globes are a pale lilac so they blend in well without being too dominant, and I leave them to fade naturally. Autumn gales dislodge the browning seedheads from their pale stalks so that they bowl around the garden like footballs or like the tumbleweed of the Wild West, dropping their seeds in unplanned places. They have now seeded all over especially along the edges of the paths, delightful in their spontaneity and creating unlikely pairings with other plants.

There are two more pairs of balancing plants along this long cross path. Twin *Eleagnus* 'Quicksilver' rise in height above the meadowy planting scheme, their narrow silver leaves conjuring the Mediterranean feel of olive trees, their small yellow flowers spilling out intoxicating scent in early summer. Their lemony fragrance is so strong that you can smell it from far away across the field. This hardy shrub, which is wind- and coast-tolerant, has only one downside, which is that it suckers. This is more likely to happen if the roots are disturbed, so where possible I avoid hoeing or digging near it. When I do find suckers, I pot them up, and from this decided to experiment with growing them long-term in containers. A pair of eleagnus have now been in large terracotta pots either side of the front door for four years, where their graceful silver leaves look soft against the stonework, their winter branches a place for strings of white lights. They do flower but not extensively because of needing some light pruning to keep them to the right size. When they had filled the pots with their roots I took them out, used an old handsaw to cut off the bottom quarter of rootball and repotted on top of fresh compost. They have even tolerated sharing the pots with a grass, the fluid lines of New Zealand wind grass, *Anemanthele lessoiana*, making the experiment a success all round.

The other pair of plants to give weight and balance to the long path is of yew, and these grow close to the woodland border at the west end of the Flower Garden. They are two large cubes with pyramids on top, difficult to get the angles right during the annual clipping but shapes that I particularly enjoy for their sharp-edged contrast to the relaxed perennials. They also have a story behind how they came to be this shape. There were stone pillars to either side of a gate at Chesters Walled Garden and these were topped with pyramid finials set on cubes. Finding a couple of yew seedlings that had germinated in the borders, I planted them in front of the pillars and began training them in a humorous echo of the finials. When we started making our new garden they were only a couple of feet tall, but I grew them on and they are now chest height, dark green and solid in their bulk, strong counterpoints to the free and easy perennials.

It is these static shapes and strong lines of paths and edges that allow the planting to have free rein. It's a classic combination in an English garden to have an underlying formality that underpins informality. But this is given a contemporary slant by the sheer size of the borders in the Flower Garden and their link to, and exaggerated imitation of, the hay meadows of the North Pennines. In winter, this layout becomes much more visible – and something that I appreciate for its calm – but in summer, it is a framework within which the garden can expand. Creating that framework was one of the hardest jobs that we did, days when our backs and muscles ached and we felt disheartened by the sheer amount of work. The plants, though, needed homes, *The English Garden* needed monthly copy and the garden took on a momentum of its own.

Constructing the Layout

In summer when the borders are ebullient and exuberant, they rise and fall around the central pivot of the yew domes. These, and the underlying rhythms of the few simple paths, allow the planting free rein, contained as it is without a framework. It's similar to the way that a mown path through a meadow enhances and counterpoints the freedom of grasses and flowers. Laying out the paths and constructing the hard landscaping elements of the garden was relentlessly hard work. My diary describes a day of rain that allowed me to catch up with emails and filing, of the relief in having a less physical day with a massage booked to unlock "my dreadfully overworked, stiff and knotted muscles after months of hard graft and heaving watering cans, lugging hosepipes and carrying heavy things."

Thanks to the genius idea of using the digger to sift out rocks, some of the backbreaking work had been saved, but it still left weeks of stone picking and forking through the soil to get rid of roots. There was a constant round of hoeing to keep on top of the green fuzz of germinating weeds, their previously buried seeds now kicked into life by being brought to the surface. My elbows were jarred as I hit stone after stone, taking these out and throwing them into the paths, repetitive and relentless work. In places, the digger tracks had caused compaction and the rain had then cemented it. Some years previously, when the empty house was being used as a bothy, there had been a wide track sweeping from the gate in a wide circle and out again. It had been made of a large grade of hardwearing whinstone and we were forever finding lumps of this dark grey rock as they worked their way to the surface – and still do.

Valuable help came from the two Dots, volunteers who were both coincidentally called Dot, who cheerfully helped to unpack numerous sacks and dig planting holes. The back terrace was a jumble of bags, trays, pots, barrows and reused hop sacks full of peonies, asters or geums. Every incursion into it helped to make it less chaotic. Geranium expert Robin Moss brought gifts of his favourite plants that we must have: the blackest phaeums, the best reds, the palest blues, the bluest blues, all delights. Friends Barry and Eileen repaired the shed walls, heaved stones, edged new borders and made many trips to the local recycling centre. As that first spring and summer edged into a drought, we gave them lunch outside and feasted on flapjacks and tea.

The many tons of stone that we extracted from the soil – a rough estimate was over fifty tons – were put to good use in laying the foundation for the paths. To make the division between border soil and path we used the cheapest boards known as sarking boards, rough sawn softwood usually used in roof construction. David fastened these to square wooden pegs set at intervals. We filled the space within these edging boards with the stones, laying them like a jigsaw puzzle with the top side as flat as possible. It felt satisfying to take random shapes and fit them together to form the bottom level of a path that we would be able to walk on in the future. On top of this patchwork of rocks we laid hardcore, a limestone sub-base sometimes known as crusher run. The top layer of gravel only went on once we had the borders in place, the greenhouse up and had finished the messy work.

It was April the following year when we took delivery of twenty tons of gravel. It came on an enormous wagon, the driver skilfully negotiating the narrow width of cattle grid and gate and reversing to above the steps to the front door. That way we would have less distance to wheelbarrow it. Self-binding gravel from the Raisby quarry just outside Durham, it poured like liquid gold from the back of the tipped-up truck, forming an enormous heap. David had been inspired by seeing it at Belsay Hall, an English Heritage property in Northumberland, whilst on a heritage skills course in lime mortar.

Hardwearing and of even and fine quality, this gravel has a high content of what are called fines or quarry dust. This means that it stays firmer under foot than loose gravels.

Self-binding gravel mellows and ages well, the light tone matching the paler stones that make up the mix of colours in the house walls and looking as though the sun is shining even on a dull day. Shadows lie crisply across its mellow surface, not broken up as they are with washed gravel. By the end of this process, the depth of the path was about eight inches, firm for the trundling of wheelbarrows yet easy for hoeing, draining perfectly in prolonged wet weather. It is a delight to rake leaves from its regular surface in autumn, the springbok rake leaving gentle parallel lines, a therapeutic task with its regular motion, a mindful moment.

It took us nearly a year to get through the twenty-ton heap because of the preparation work involved in making the base for the paths. The final and longest job was in making the drive. Someone had previously created a rough, hard surface of old building waste, which appeared to be brick and slag, but this was all mixed in with soil, unpleasant and muddy, holding pools of water after heavy rain. We could have hired a digger but decided to do the work ourselves. It took three months, David attacking it using pickaxe and pinch bar (a large metal bar invaluable for fencing and/or breaking up compaction). I would hunker down, extracting the lumps of material to recycle them in the bottom of a twelve-inch-deep trench, before carting the soil away. Large lumps of builders' waste needed breaking up with a mel and we found all manner of buried rubbish. By hand-working the area, we could go tightly up against the low retaining wall of the Flower Garden, but it was a bit crazy doing it all ourselves.

With the rubble relaid in the bottom of the trench, we put the same layer of sub-base as the garden paths and topped that with the lovely rich gold of Raisby gravel. This completed the transformation from an ugly hotchpotch of brick, slag and mud into a beautiful uniform drive. Most important of all in the practical sense, it drained perfectly after a thunderstorm. We could then bring the car in across the cattle grid when there were cows in the field; they love to rub themselves against anything that sticks out such as wing mirrors.

The area that had been a driveway in front of the house now became a linking area between the terrace and the Flower Garden. The same gravel continued along, though this time we did not need to do all the hard work of sifting through and making a deep trench for the rubble. Like laying a new carpet, the whole unattractive mess was covered up, first with landscaping membrane, then a layer of the same gravel. It was a blissfully instant transformation. Into this, we created a large offset diamond to reference the one at the central point of the Vegetable Garden. It is made from cobbles as a nod to local cobbled farmyards, just one course deep, within which is clipped lavender 'Hidcote' surrounding a round galvanised container for annuals.

A further and smaller diamond has a centre of white mossy saxifrage and both shapes have been made using cobbles from favourite landscapes: from the Lake District, the Scottish Borders, the Northumberland coast. I have to keep them free of moss using a patio scraping tool in order to see the rounded shapes, the blue and the buff colours of the stones. The lavenders have, over the years, seeded themselves into the area around them, gravel being such a happy medium for self-seeding plants from warm countries such as verbena, dianthus, aubrietia and California poppy. This vibrant annual began with a 50p packet of seed and has multiplied and spread over the years, moving eastwards thanks to the westerly winds from its original position. Day-glow orange, the silky petals unfurl from pointed cones to flare open on hot days, attracting a range of insects. The plump pollen sacks of honeybees are bright orange. I wish I'd known about California poppies as a child. They are so spontaneous and easy, fast to grow, with their little pixie hats that children can lift from the unfurling petals.

We have had to decide whether or not to leave the self-seeded lavenders. They do break up the area, changing the effect, but I find it hard to take them out. They are all true to the original 'Hidcote', that serene summer colour of deep purple, dense and compact. Some have been moved to the Vegetable Garden to make a scented edge to the path to the compost heap; even though they have rooted through the membrane, they are easy enough to take out without damage. But mostly, I allow them to be.

For years, I have taught as well as written in magazines that you shouldn't cut into the old wood when pruning lavender, but with so many self-sown 'Hidcotes' I could afford to be a bit cavalier with them. When it came to re-gravelling the paths – a big job usefully undertaken during lockdown – it was quicker to cut them back hard in order to rake the new gravel around them. One in particular had seeded itself amongst white violas and David felt that it spoilt the effect. Not wanting to dig it up and bring soil to the surface, I used loppers on the old wood of an inch in diameter, slicing all the branches to ground level and sure that this would kill it. In spring, it regrew healthy and vital, proving that it is always worth challenging accepted ideas when gardening.

The other self-seeder in the front gravel is the delightfully named fairy foxglove, *Erinus alpinus*. Tradition has it that this diminutive plant grows wherever the Romans occupied the land. It certainly does grow in the old stone walls of cottages and large country houses close to Hadrian's Wall and was plentiful in the walled garden at Chesters. It likes to grow in the nooks and tiny spaces where mortar has crumbled or between steps and paving. I brought a number of plants with me and allowed them to scatter their seed where they liked. This turned out to be the gravel area in particular, though I have also poked young plants between gaps in the paving stones of the back terrace. Semi-evergreen, this pretty little perennial has neat rosettes of leaves from which rise clusters of pale purple flowers, making it ideal for alpine troughs and containers. From the original dozen plants there are now hundreds, giving that feeling of age that you get around old cottage gardens.

The very last piece of the garden jigsaw to be put in place was something to link the terrace steps with the steps up into the Flower Garden. In this expanse of gravel, I wanted a suitable stone urn or trough and happened upon a square stone planter in a barn selling old tools and ornaments attached to an open garden in the Eden Valley. It was just the right size and shape, and to set it off we placed around it four grey-lichened deep stone slabs that I'd found propped up against the back wall and always wanted to use in some way. It created just the right bridge between house and garden. To either side of it are now a series of smaller box domes that echo the large yew domes. From the kitchen window, the line of mounds of box can be seen at the same time as the four yews. They give me great satisfaction, especially when the light catches their curved flanks.

It was satisfying too to demolish the ugly structures that we found when we came here – especially a dilapidated and bark-peeling rustic fence and a wonky barbecue made of grey concrete breeze blocks. The fence enclosed the sunken oil tank and septic tank but with rebuilt dry-stone walls, cattle grid and gate it was no longer necessary to protect them from the stock. Using a jemmy, David levered apart the unattractive fence and cleared the mound of rubble, soil and plastic that littered the surface. As a working area that we'd need access to, a solution was to use ground-covering plants in a contrasting gravel. To create distinction between the two, between local river-washed gravel and the smoother self-binding gravel, David laid a line of walling stone. Rectangular stones, irregular in size but similar enough to make a good edge, they were all of the place and fitted with the idea of keeping everything simple in terms of materials: that the garden would be made of stone, wood and plants.

Out of necessity came a gravel garden. The dome of the oil tank and the surfboard shape of the septic tank were disguised by spreads of geraniums and *Persicaria affinis*, happily rooting through the gravel whilst also preventing weeds. The gravel flows on towards the house, simply planted with just two elements: *Sisyrinchium striatum* for its spires of creamy yellow flowers and fans of iris-like leaves, and bright orange California poppies. In front of the house are small alpine plants. Thymes, saxifrages, thrift, violas and the perennial wallflower 'Constant Cheer', well-named for its orange-purple long-lasting succession of flowers. There are emerald green cushions of *Draba aizoides*, which blooms very early in the year and is covered in sharply yellow flowers. Known as alpine whitlow-grass, it needs excellent drainage such as in a scree garden or a rock bank, but here in the gravel area it is perfectly happy. The gravel bed widens out near the main gate. One of the last areas to be developed, it was where we had lined out assorted categories of useful stone as we made the garden. One day, needing somewhere to prop myself and enjoy a cup of tea, I balanced a plank in the corner that I had noticed was sheltered from the prevailing wind by a slight kink in the dry-stone wall. This was going to be the best spot for a bench, arched over by a leaning hawthorn whose silver lichened branches I could look up into to watch robin and blackbird.

The stone was moved, the area levelled, a lovely wooden bench set facing the sun, and I chose plants that would give a see-through screen, a sense of enclosure but within being boxed in. Gently waving wands of the ornamental grass *Molinia* 'Transparent', delicate canary-yellow racemes of tree lupin, lilac alliums, verbena and the scented evening primrose, *Oenethera stricta*. Attracting plenty of insect life, I added to them with the prickly sea holly, *Eryngium* 'Silver Ghost' and the punchy red-pink wands of *Dianthus carthusianorum*, a tall dianthus that self-seeds. I could now sit on the bench looking out across the fullness of the garden through a loose veil of flower stems, the air alive with insects.

These are all plants that revel in their gravel footing and will seed themselves, even the Molinia grass. It is easy to hoe the river gravel to keep them in check, or I pot up youngsters to give to friends, just as I was given seeds of the evening primrose from a French garden some years back. The gravel formed a unified background, a pleasure to walk on, and covered up any remnants of unattractive rubble. Other areas followed the same theme. An odd triangle between path and wall, an alpine bed, a narrow south-facing border in front of a low wall where I grow just houseleeks, all topped in river gravel but separated from the self-binding gravel by a thin line of stone. It's a subtle distinction that plays with slightly different textures, colours and sizes of stone.

Over two years we had worked relentlessly, helped by volunteers with the planting but moving all the heavy materials ourselves: boulders to make steps and edgings, the many tons of stone to line the paths, twenty tons of limestone sub-base, twenty tons of golden gravel and ten tons of contrasting river gravel for the borders. It was physically tiring work, something I threw myself into so I could focus on the future rather than what I had left behind. At times I felt overloaded by the sheer amount of work, with battling hard compacted soil and creeping thistle, with lugging boulders, pruning, sawing, dragging, barrowing, hauling hosepipes, keeping motivation going. In my diary I wrote, "I feel

I've reached the limit of my endurance tonight. Three days of tough work, digging, lifting, grappling with claggy soil and I feel bruised and aching. The soil is sticky with winter wet, my boots and spades heavy, my shoulders jarred by stones. How will I have the energy to start again tomorrow?"

I have worked outdoors all my life. That is apart from a brief and miserable few months in a smoke-filled office (those were the days of cigarettes in the workplace and I shared a small room with a chain-smoker). It has been hard work but has given me a deep sense of the seasons, an awareness and appreciation of changes in weather. By being so used to qualities of light, I can always tell the time to within a few minutes, day and night. There have sometimes been trips to the physio – a pulled back or shoulder – but keeping moving has avoided the physical problems that come with sitting and being too static. What has suffered is my skin, probably from the earlier years of landscaping and garden maintenance when I didn't regularly use suntan creams. Now I always wear a hat, though it is a bit too late to prevent sun-damaged skin. As a woman working in horticulture, my career has had its ups and downs, but making this new garden in my late fifties, putting in sometimes nine-hour days, was very demanding.

After that first tough year of making the new garden, I needed a break and went to the Buddhist monastery of Samye Ling in the Borders for three days. Either side of the winding road up Eskdalemuir, the hills looked soft in overcast summer light. It was then a surprise to see the gold roof a Tibetan temple emerging from a Scottish forest, and at the gates a white stupa with fluttering prayer flags. I collected my key from the friendly monk who was Guest Master, went to my room and flaked out on the bed. I couldn't believe it when I woke some hours later but I was utterly exhausted. I slept on and off for much of the next two days, surprising myself at the depth of my tiredness, mentally and physically worn out from two stressful years and unremitting hard work. I didn't even mind the peacocks shrieking at dawn. By day three, I felt able to communicate and volunteered to work in the monastery garden, scything nettles and docks from the hedge bottom (how very familiar!) and working amongst the massed rows of orange calendulas for healing and decoration. Taking home with me a collection of rounded cobbles, they would eventually be incorporated into the diamond shape in gravel and surround the bed of 'Hidcote' lavenders.

I suppose that we went at it full tilt for several reasons: needing to quickly establish the plants in their new soil, to provide material on a monthly basis for my column in *The English Garden*, and to provide a focus for the future and recovery from the loss of Chesters. Since then, it has been at a better pace. You can build far more endurance into gardening if you alternate jobs so that you are using different muscles from shorter stints at using hedging shears, spade or secateurs. It helps to avoid repetitive strain and the variety is more interesting. Warming up with some yoga or stretching helps to prevent injury – twenty minutes every morning pays off. It is especially important after winter if you haven't been doing very much for some months – though I really enjoy getting out in those winter months, helped by the myth that I might be getting ahead. I've found the best way is to walk after gardening as the rhythm and the movement keep me from having back ache. But as Monty Don often says on *Gardeners' World*, there's no point in creating a garden if you don't take the time to sit and look.

In mid-October, when David was out on the fells riding a friend's horse, I decided to take full enjoyment of a gorgeous day. I read a book on the front bench under a sun that was hot at 9.30 in the morning. Wearing T-shirt, straw hat and sandals, I wandered slowly, taking in the different angles of the garden and looking at the details. The asters were crowded with insects – hoverflies, but-terflies, bees – and there seemed one insect for every bloom, the air shimmering with back-lit wings. I sat in the wicker chair in the greenhouse with our cat on my lap and ate tomatoes sweet off the vine as bees bobbed noisily against the roof glass. I squeezed rosemary for its pungent sticky scent and the menthol leaves of Balm of Gilead. I took the picnic rug onto the lawn, propped my head on a cushion and shading my eyes with my hat, drifted off. Blue sky, long-tailed tits calling restlessly, warmth on my skin and the sound of the river. It was all worthwhile.

Water: the Burn and the River

We can hear the river and burn that flows into it throughout day and night, sometimes a soft background murmur, sometimes awesomely loud. The burn flows just six metres from the house. From the desk where I write – my father's old leather-topped keyhole desk – I can look down onto it and see the river too, away to the right. This window faces west across a field to a dark conifer wood, once a cash crop of Christmas trees that was never felled, and a thick, dark, quiet place for roe deer and tawny owls. Sometimes I watch the deer as they walk slowly up from the East Allen, unaware that I can see them. When they reach the barbed wire fence, they gracefully leap it from a standing start to slip in between the spruce trees.

From my window, the burn makes a shallow curve between low grassy banks before running beneath a footbridge, alongside our garden wall and into the river. When we came here, its passage was choked with debris and overhanging trees so we pruned the low branches of hawthorn and willow to get a clearer flow. I'm glad we had listened to the forecast as the next day was one of heavy rain and it was good to see the stream rushing under the footbridge and on, unimpeded by the branches we'd just cut back.

The boundary wall by the stream was all tumbled down, as were many of the garden walls, so David took it apart to re-build it. He taught himself how to dry-stone wall, using a book from the library, but for a first try, the drop to the burn made it particularly challenging. Working away, with his back to the water, he sometimes heard splashing behind him. It took him a while to register what it was. When he realised, he called me excitedly, in time to see a large fish making its way up the burn to spawn. We thought then it was salmon but later learnt that, although salmon will use the main river, it is sea trout that migrate up this little burn.

It has become a regular thing, looking for the sea trout after an autumn spate, usually at the end of October, beginning of November. Friends ask to be told when they are on the move so that they too can watch. Sometimes the rain is heaviest in the night and we miss much of it, but it generally happens over a few days. It was that first time, though, that was the most special. It was thrilling to see these great fish, their bodies half out of the water, slithering like eels across the shallow few inches of depth at the tractor ford. I followed them as they forced their muscular way up waterfalls and rapids, or lay up to recover for some minutes before tackling the next obstacle.

In a half crouch – though I didn't know how well I could be seen through the current – I traced the passage of a large sea trout and then flattened myself on the bank where the stream nearly enters Squirrel Wood. After that it becomes steeper and choked with fallen timber. The fish came to a place that was a bit calmer and I watched her – a female is known as a hen – thrashing a redd in the gravel by lying on her side and using her tail to wiggle a slight trough in which to lay her eggs. A cock fish – smaller than her – waited alongside as she laid her eggs, squirming and tail flicking as he released his milky sperm. She then moved slightly upstream before thrashing her tail to cover the eggs with gravel. I found it quite amazing that all this was happening just a short stretch from our garden wall.

Sea trout run up smaller streams than salmon and occupy a different environmental niche to them, though they do compete in some larger rivers for spawning grounds. In the pulsing waters of the stream, they can be quite hard to spot. Polished boulders glint like a fish's back. As I stare, shadows and shapes in the current can look like trout until the water suddenly morphs into an angular fin.

Water: the Burn and the River

By the second year, I knew to watch out for their migration. After a rainy night, it was a sodden wet day, one of those days when the countryside is seen through a filter of blurred grey and the light leaves quickly by four o'clock. The sea trout had been waiting for such a day when they were able to get up the steep rise from the main river. They came, wriggling and slapping, tails like sharks' fins cutting through the water, pausing and regathering strength before threshing again upstream. I phoned the poet (and geranium man) Robin Moss who had asked for an alert. He walked here, though he doesn't like bad weather, repeatedly moving his head to knock the raindrops from his cap. We watched together as several fish worked their way up towards the redding pool just below the pine wood. Thrilling.

There was such heavy rain that night that before going to bed I went out to the footbridge with my torch to see how high the burn was. It still had three feet to go to reach the bridge, the water thundering over the waterfall like a millrace, a chute of brown pounding into the pool below. By morning, it had dropped again and the power had gone out of the burn. There was no sign of the sea trout who had used the high water level to migrate up under cover of dark and free of daytime predators such as herons.

The burn gathers water from the high moors to the south of our valley. From below the two Allendale chimneys, it drops nearly a thousand feet. Although it has never flooded the garden, it can be very dramatic when in spate, either in the sudden rise of a summer thunderstorm or the day-by-day saturation of relentless winter rain. When it comes charging down and reaches a certain speed and fullness, it is exhilarating and scary to hear the grinding of boulders. Rumbling and reverberating as they are bowled along in the current, they are then left behind in an altered stream-bed when the level drops.

In 2011, when we had only lived here for eighteen months, a huge deluge carved out a section of the bank just above where the burn joins the main river. We were alarmed to see the high voltage cable of our electricity supply protruding from the exposed soil – key to the timeless look of the old stone house is the lack of visible telephone or electricity cables. There followed a week of bizarre sights as a steampunk of a machine lumbered down the track and red and white roadwork barriers were erected around a hole in the field, to the fascination of the cattle. On one side of our garden wall, David was lifting potatoes; on the other, the machine began boring deep beneath the field and heading for the East Allen. A similar square hole had been made on the opposite bank.

As the Ditch Witch, as it was called, laboured to drill through boulders, there was a moment when the strangeness was added to by a workman in bright yellow plastic waders, his ankles and waist secured with yellow tape, reaching the middle of the Allen holding a sensor that could trace the drill under the river bed. A black plastic pipe was then threaded through the tunnel through which our electric supply would run. The second phase was to drill beneath the burn and in less than two hours, the garden began to heave and the drill split the ground as if the machine were a giant mole. The tungsten carbide head had cut through rock and boulders. The men had manoeuvred huge coils of pipe, being careful not to damage our box hedge. We were in awe of the whole job and of the river that has such destructive power. The end of that hot day was like Canarian weather. There were vast numbers of insects in the air – a pity that the swallows had left – and bees and butterflies crowded on the sedums and asters. The machines departed and I became extra aware of the sounds of long-tailed tits calling, of pheasants, a distant quad bike and the tinkling of the now quiet stream.

Water: the Burn and the River

Under snow, the burn becomes a dark line threading through its banks. When it turns really cold, trailing branches accumulate ice, formed into globules as if made by a glassblower, fat, round, misshapen and clinking in the movement of the water. One very cold winter, the burn froze over with just the occasional dark swirl in the middle where I could look down through five inches of ice to see the water flowing underneath. It then became so frozen over that were no cracks showing down into the stream, which gurgled deeply as if in a cavern. Then comes the snow melt, the water turning milky, and the burn is a tumult once more.

It's surprising then what things survive without changing. The patch of opposite leaved saxifrage, *Saxifraga oppositifolium*, fragile-looking and surely without much root system, yet there it is every spring, fresh green-yellow. In the stony edges, colts-foot, *Tussilago farfara*, blooms with its scaly, crimson stems supporting dandelion-like golden flowers. These turn to fluffy round seedheads, blowing easily in the wind and hopefully not into the garden. Perhaps it's its invasive roots that let it anchor itself into the ever-changing stream sides. It flowers without leaves; these grow later, grey-green and silver-haired, vaguely horseshoe-shaped, hence its name. The botanical name *Tussilago* reflects this traditional herbal use, "tussis" meaning "cough". It was prepared as syrups and tinctures for sore throats, asthma and chest infections, but as coltsfoot contains pyrrolizidine alkaloids it is now not recommended to be taken internally.

A plant that is really tough, withstanding the tugging of the stream in spate, is woodrush, *Luzula sylvatica*. This is the ever-green rush that carpets the woods, its broad dark green leaves thick and lush, its delicately drooping brown flowers like fine tassels. Woodrush makes dense tussocks and we've found this tough and durable plant good for stabilising banks. I use it to edge a flower bed of hellebores, pink cow parsley and the butterbur

Petasites hybridus, because it can be chopped and hacked and made to create a solid green ribbon between border and path. I also grow a form of woodrush that has a fine silver line round each leaf, *Luzula sylvatica* 'Marginata', which will also grow well in containers.

Another native plant that helps to bind sloping ground is yellow flag, *Iris pseudacorus*. Its solid, thick rhizomes are tough and fibrous, making a hard mat of roots that water flows over. I grow yellow flag in the flower borders, a link between garden and landscape, blurring the lines between the wild and the cultivated. It's a beauty in spring, the wide leaves bringing texture and upward movement amongst the mass of perennials, the flowers golden yellow with curving falling petals. Depending on which part of the plant is used, yellow flag can be used to produce natural dyes. In Scotland, the leaves were used to make a bright green for tartan and tweed. Depending on the mordant used, leaves give a range of colours from pale yellow to bright or dark green. Mordants are binding agents, with a number of different minerals being used to adhere to both fibre and dye so the colour doesn't fade. Which you use – tin, copper, iron, alum or chrome – will determine what colour you get.

Tree planting is of course one of the best ways of stabilising the banks and when I find seedlings of hawthorn, I add them to the top of the retaining wall by the burn. When we began gardening here, I had brought a mass of snowdrops with me and some of these I planted in the soil on the top of the footbridge abutment. It was a natural place to put them, so when they flowered in late January, I was pleased to see that there were lots of snowdrops already in the wide sloping bank between the burn and our garden wall. It gave a sense of continuity that some previous owner, decades before, had also seen it as the right place to plant snowdrops.

Water: the Burn and the River

Later on in spring, the woods in Allendale are full of wild garlic or ransoms, *Allium ursinum*, and this grows where the burn meets the river. With wide flat leaves, it comes up through deposited silt, through leafmould and amongst tree roots, fresh and green and delicious in soups, salads, pesto and curries. At the same time of year, there are leaves of lords and ladies so it's important not to get these confused. Lords and ladies, *Arum maculatum*, are poisonous, their leaves more arrowhead-shaped than the garlic. I grow it in my woodland border for its orange-red autumn berries.

When wild garlic blooms, the woods sparkle with light from the thousands of white starry flowers. Like the leaves, they are edible, and we use the individual florets on salads. When the plant dies back in late spring, as the leaf canopy denies it light and the garlic's moment of exuberance is over, there's an intense and pungent onion smell. It's a plant of old woodland, and some of the woods near our house are designated semi-ancient. I know that wild garlic grows throughout Britain but to me it's a plant of the north.

Of these wild plants along the burn, the only one that I don't grow in my garden is wild garlic. It seeds itself too freely and would take over (I have experience from a previous garden!). Although the stone walls define the boundary of the garden, wildlife and wild plants live on both sides, and I enjoy the continuum of this flow. Red campion, ragged robin, ferns and primroses grow on either side of the human-imposed line. Birds come and go over the line, but one that is entirely of the world of water is the dipper.

A bird of these northern fast-flowing rivers, the dipper *Cinclus cinclus* is our only aquatic songbird. Plump and chocolate-brown, this delightful bird has a white throat and breast that flashes like a semaphore signal when it bobs up and down on a midstream rock. You can tell its favourite boulders because they are white-splashed with droppings. From these lookout posts, they slip into the river to feed underwater on aquatic invertebrates, particularly caddis fly larva and mayfly nymphs. No matter how often I watch them – and I see them almost every day – I am always fascinated by their ability to move on the river bed in a kind of half-walk, half-swim motion. Their sweet warbling seems of the river, a fluid song that carries over the sound of water and that, sung throughout the year, will cheer me in the middle of winter. Dippers feed in the main river but also up the side streams, and one will often pass under the bridge, flying fast along the burn, uttering a piping alarm call if it sees me.

As the burn drops in a dry spell and I can see the new shape of its course, the driftwood wedged between boulders, the gravelly sandy bed, I go down there with my sketchbook. Isolating a square using lengths of field rush stems, I draw anything within it. I suppose it's a nod back to when I worked as a site planner in archaeology, drawing everything within a metre square frame, or in botanical surveys when plants are sampled within a quadrat. The drawings that I make – of bark, lawn or gravel – are about texture devoid of any outside reference, a focus on the material. Using a black ink pen, as I once did on drafting film on Roman digs, I note each pebble, rounded or irregular, fragments of bark or stems, grains of sand and gravel. It's a calming, mindful process.

As I draw, there's a scent of mint from where I've crushed the plant on the stream edge. Water mint has a scent more like chocolate mints than peppermint. It grows amongst the field rush, its tenacious runners spreading in the silty earth, mauve flowers growing in whorls on its reddish square stems. The hairy, oval, aromatic leaves can be used in drinks, and it is a native plant that is a good choice for wildlife ponds.

Out of the corner of my eye, I notice a grey squirrel racing along the boundary wall behind me. This wall, the one that runs all the way along the western edge of our garden and down to the East Allen, is the squirrels' corridor, a high line for getting between the woods on either side of the river. The squirrels leap across the gap at the footbridge, nimbly run along a willow wattle panel and up a large ash tree that overhangs the river. From here, it's an easy leap onto the trees on the opposite bank. When we came here fourteen years ago, Squirrel Wood – a local name that isn't on any map – referred to red squirrels and we had a couple of sightings of beautiful native reds. Once we started to see greys, there were no more reds, due to a combination of competition for food and squirrel pox virus.

There are still reds in the East Allen Valley, not far away in the Deneholme woods at Allendale Town. As you travel up the Allen Valley, there are various places where red squirrels can be found, but my favourite spot is Old Man Bottom. There's no apostrophe to Man, and local people like to correct anyone who spells it wrongly. 'Old Man' was a common informal name for a mine, so there may be some connection with lead mining. It's a favourite picnic and paddling spot for many, where a faded blue footbridge spans the Allen on tall supports to allow for when the river is in spate. A painted wooden gauge stands in the centre of the ford with a sign that warns "Caution – Due to scouring depths may be deeper than indicated".

A wide grassy lawn is a summer's day picnic place, the turf bright with mountain pansies. Despite its botanical name of *Viola lutea* (*"lutea"* meaning "yellow"), these bonny pansies are very variable, ranging from yellow to mauve or purple, purple shades being more usual. They're a typical plant of calaminarian grassland, able to grow on metal-rich soils, as in this valley, which was mined for its lead, zinc and silver. In the Scots pine wood, with its feeling of openness and regularly spaced trunks, it's possible to see red squirrels, fluid and lithe as they run up and down the tree trunks.

Second Nature

This place makes me think of the Hundred Acre Wood of *Winnie the Pooh*. Scots pines, thinned out some years back, have furrowed boles that are bare and straight. They turn ruddy brown towards the crowns from which swoop graceful dark branches. Sunlight filters between the trees, flecking the mossy woodland floor and turning it yellow-green. There are waist-high fronds of male fern and the ground is spongy with needles.

I pick up the remnants of a pine cone. It has been efficiently deconstructed, the scales chewed apart to extract the seeds, a sign of feeding squirrels. These female cones start tightly closed and emerald green. They take two to three years to develop until dispersal stage when their ripe contents fall to the ground. Take a cone indoors and the warmth of the house will make it expand so the winged seeds can be tapped out.

The sound of my footsteps is absorbed by the springy mass of needles so I can move quietly through the wood. I hear the high-pitched calls of goldcrests though I can't spot them. They move restlessly through the treetops, using their thin beaks to pick insects out from between the pairs of pine needles. There's the sudden clatter of distress calls, with an answering sharp "kee-wick", as small birds mob a tawny owl. A screech of jays, a woodpecker call, but so far no red squirrels.

Domes of fly agaric, scarlet with flaky white spots, have been scraped by teeth marks. Though toxic to humans, reds are able to eat these storybook fungi, often leaving them to dry on a high branch before adding to their winter stash. A scratching sound on dry bark makes me look up and, there they are, two squirrels chasing helter-skelter around a nearby trunk, auburn fur glowing in a patch of light. There's an exuberance to their movements as they spiral up and down, oblivious to my presence in the energy of the moment. Their hold here may be fragile, but I'm happy knowing that it's still possible to see red squirrels in the Allen Valley, even if they no longer come to our garden.

Red squirrels came frequently to the bird nuts during my time at Chesters Walled Garden. Visitors would watch them from the nursery area, amazed at how close they could stand, amazed too by the confidence of the greater spotted woodpeckers and the many nuthatches – the record was seven nuthatches on the feeder at once. If I went in the woods to collect leafmould, the squirrels would show their annoyance that I was on their patch by tail flicking and making a whirring, squeaking sound. I loved to watch them run so lightly along the branches of the beech trees that they seemed to float along them, the light catching the beautiful russet of their fur. They are so much more delicate and light than the greys, which are chunkier and more muscular. It was the end for the red squirrels at Chesters when I saw one that had strange pustules above its eye. Squirrel pox virus was just beginning to hit the news and it was with great sadness that I realised what it meant.

We become so used to losses from the natural world but there is good news too. On the fine gravel of the East Allen, not far from our garden, there are footprints. And beneath the bridge by our house, on a large raised stone, are dark droppings studded with fragments of bone – otter spraint. To check, I shimmy under the bridge and crumble the spraint between my fingers; an earthy, slightly fragrant smell that has often been compared to jasmine tea and it's a pretty good description. I find it incredible that otters have been here in the dark, just a few feet from our kitchen window. The spraint is a scent marking and they like to do this in obvious places; these are otter landmarks, often used over many years. Favourite stones may go green with algae over time because of the nutrients that the otter deposits in its droppings, but this stone gets washed clean every time there's a rise in water level.

I have yet to see these mysterious otters that slip by in the night, though I have just once heard one whistle. I've seen otters on the South Tyne, once at three o'clock in the afternoon, but the closest I've been to them has been in Scotland. Staying in early autumn in a black painted fisherman's cottage by the Findhorn, I walked before breakfast along the river bank. Hearing that unmistakeable whistling, I stooped down so I was hidden by scrub and could follow a mother and two cubs for some twenty minutes as they tumbled fluidly over each other, half play, half hunting. They turned stones over, rolling them with their paws. I was so close I could see into pink mouths and teeth. Next morning I found the holt, which was between the massive rocks of the bridge abutment, and could watch them daily.

On Islay, I picked up a number of ticks from lying above a cove to watch otters at the sea's edge. On Arran, I watched an otter eating a fish on the tiny island of a rock surrounded by water down which the moon shone a long path in Lamlash Bay. Despite the many times I have looked over the river wall at our house or gone quietly to the bridge, I have never seen the otters that I know to be there.

Using Stone:
Inspiration from Landscape

The place under the bridge where we see the otter spraint was laid many years ago with large rectangular stones, neatly fitted together like cobbles, all set in the direction of water flow. It's been so well made that this is the only part of the stream bed that doesn't change its shape after a flood. It gives me pleasure to look at it, to see the skilful way that the individual stones have been tightly knitted together. There are other places in the valley where stone is similarly used and each time I pass them when out on a walk, I appreciate what went into the work. In Allen Mills Wood, a streamlet is channelled with stones forming sloping sides that overlay a cobbled bottom so that the base is never damaged in heavy rain. It's such a simple idea but so beautifully executed, perhaps back in the lead mining days.

At the other end of the valley, two very steep roads descend to a narrow bridge, a single span high above a ravine formed by the East Allen: one bank descends to it from the south and another from the north. The single track lane does a sharp dogleg over the bridge and has been the cause of a number of incidents due to people following satnav instructions. For much of the way down one side, there's a cobbled ditch, just two stones wide in the bottom, the shape of setts on a roadside. The ditch flows year round alongside a wooded bank where honeysuckle twines up hazels, a single juniper clings to the slope and the slender grass, wood melick, arches gracefully. I often wonder who made this runnel, its stones rhythmical as is the sound that they give to the water, so pragmatic and beautiful.

All around the Allen Valleys – and in the wider North Pennines – are examples of beauty in practical solutions. Farmyards that are a mixture of flags and cobbles have an honesty of design that comes from their functional use. The stones, gathered when field clearing or taken from the rivers, are used in patterns less intended to be decorative than to be serviceable. Larger stones may be used as immovable borders, smaller cobbles covering the surface of yards and barn floors, but with stones laid in channels for drainage. What results has an arts and crafts directness and sympathy with its surroundings – and an unintended beauty.

We've picked up on these thoughts in the way we've used stone in the garden. First instinctively, then more by design. The way that these stones have been used locally and their unknowable history is echoed in the garden. It is in the placing of one stone against another, taken from the valley and not imported or bought from a builder's merchant, that has a link with land and a relationship that is fitting. Shortly after moving here, David went on a one-day course in laying cobbles that was run by the Heritage Skills Initiative. He learnt how to select stones that had a flat face on one side but a depth to them so that, when placed tightly side by side, they sank into a bed of sand or sub-soil like a dental diagram of teeth. Traditionally, it is worn river stones that are used and we found plenty in the garden as we turned over soil that hadn't been worked for forty years. I enjoy the difference of shapes and sizes and the unevenness that is transformed into a pattern when multiplied over an area. Cobble stones should be packed closely together and the gaps between them filled with the base material. Traditionally, no setting limes or cements are used. I would have liked to cobble the paths around our old stone house to fit in with what I'd seen in the yards of local farms but it was just too much work. We were too busy making the garden, so cobbles were used selectively between house and terrace, and the paths made from the self-binding gravel. Maybe one day we will have the time and the energy to do more.

It was natural to want to use stone as much as possible in making the garden. Our house is built from sandstone, quarried locally, but there are also river stones incorporated into its walls. There's a range of colours from pale biscuit to dark honey. All the mortar is lime-based so that the walls are breathable – it makes them feel alive, knowing that. The effect, with this sandy lime pointing, is soft, a suitable backdrop for the garden. Tree shadows fall in broken waves across the surface. On cold days, the stonework feels light and welcoming. On late sunny evenings, the walls glow. I love the irregularity of the sizes of the stones, the way that there are occasional small thin in-fillers set vertically, the odd grey river stones, the uneven surfaces. Those around the front door feel monumental, smoother for being worked to shape, the lintel scored by chisel blows.

That the roof is also made of stone makes the whole house feel part of the landscape. The roof slabs are graded from the largest just above the eaves up to slimmer rows along the top, the apex a line of triangular ridging stones. Mosses and lichens colonise the stone, adding a further range of textures and colours. Bats live beneath the slabs much of the year, leaving for their winter roosts when the weather turns cold. I've no way of checking this but a logical place for them to stay is in the tunnels of nearby old mine workings where there's a constant temperature. In summer, it must get very hot under the heat-absorbent roof, but they return every year.

It was a while before I realised in that first summer that the faint scrabbling noise above the bedroom ceiling was not mice but bats. The room is open to the great oak beams, and as we lay one morning half-awake, David asked me "Can you hear the bats?" In my sleepy state, I murmured, "How lovely." I find the sounds of the bats very soothing; as they return from their night's foraging, I can hear the light tap-tapping sound that their wings make as they work their way along beneath the roof stones. It's curiously reassuring to know that they live alongside us, also needing to eat, to be sheltered, to sleep and to find warmth. It's wonderful to be woken at dawn by a young owl sitting on the roof above the bedroom window and wanting to be fed. And to then sit on the window seat watching the bats coming home. They get noisier towards the end of summer and I think of the young bats coming in clumsily like teenagers after a night out.

Intrigued by the bats, we ask for help from Ruth from the local bat group in identifying which species they were. For a proper survey, we should really have had four people, one recording at each corner of the house, but it was an indication. As the sun set, we used bat detectors, tuning the dials to align with the frequency of a bat's call, a burst of noise that registers its inaudible sound. The first bat to emerge was a common pipistrelle, *Pipistrellus pipistrellus*, the clicking sounds it produces registering at 45kHz, and they appear about twenty minutes after sundown. We counted them out as they looped over the garden and headed off purposefully towards the fields. A faster set of clicks signalled a different frequency on the detector, and the next group were Natterer's bats, *Myotis nattereri*, that always appear some minutes after the pipistrelles. Then we heard a different set of clicks, slower and louder than the Natterer's, and Ruth said we had a whiskered bat too, *Myotis mystacinus*, confirmed by its different behaviour. As dusk deepened, we watched it fly systematically up and down in front of the house, sweeping up insects as it passed.

Of these three species, we counted some forty bats, but it was a chance remark of mine that added the fourth. I'd always noticed a slight smell in the bedroom that was really quite pleasant, like coffee grounds or the faint remnant of a curry. I don't know why

Using Stone: Inspiration from Landscape

I mentioned it, but Ruth knew straight away that we also had soprano pipistrelles, *Pipistrellus pygmaeus*. The scent is given off by their fur and they get their name because of their higher frequency echolocation call. These bats are the gardener's friend, enabling me to work in the evenings despite living by the river and the wet rushy meadows of the haugh. Each pipistrelle can eat 3,000 midges a night and people are constantly astonished that we hardly have any midges.

On the East Allen, there are also Daubenton's bats, *Myotis daubentonii*. Sometimes known as the water bat, they can scoop up insects from the surface of the water using their large feet or their tail membrane. And in the daytime, I have seen the largest of all the bats, the noctule bat, *Nyctalus noctula*, flying high and fast in a straight line over the haugh. These bats usually live in trees and have a diet of moths, beetles and winged ants. It brings the total of bat species in or very close to the garden to six, with four species having their summer quarters up there under our stone-slabbed roof, stone on stone, part of the landscape and its wildlife.

Creating a unity between house and garden is easier if you pick up on what the house is made of. When designing gardens, I keep to a maximum of three different materials; in the case of this house, it is two. Old roof slabs make stepping stones in a border, flat-topped boulders a curving path to the compost heaps, and stones are used to edge a woodland border of hellebores, grasses and ferns. I went away for a couple of days to give a lecture and as always, the garden had subtly changed in that time. There's a moment when I come back and I briefly get a new perspective on the familiar. I had imagined an informal gravel path to the greenhouse lapped over by carpeting thymes rather than edged by the wooden boarding of the rest of the borders. I returned to find that David had laid stones on either side, roughly rectangular and of good walling quality, with every fourth stone jutting into the path. The result was a delight, the effect having an arts and crafts aesthetic, and I stood there with a big smile on my face in appreciation of what he had created.

I was particularly proud of David's skill when, after some intent looking, a farming friend asked who had rebuilt the dry-stone walls. Not a professional waller, but David, and he'd made them regular and neat with no gaps that a baby rabbit might slip through. As any waller knows, the inner core of a wall should be made up of carefully placed filling stones that help bind the wall together. The end profile is an A-shape for stability, with each layer getting slightly narrower toward the top. At regular intervals, there are through stones (*thruffs*, as they are called in Northumberland) that span the width of the wall locking the two sides together. Roughly rounded coping stones are placed on top, tightly pressed up against each other and again spanning the width of the wall. There are thousands of miles of these walls running across the landscape of the North Pennines, reflecting the geology of the area and adding character as well as wildlife habitats.

The reason that many of the walls were in such a dire state when we moved here was that they had been lazily infilled with soil instead of stone. The soil had washed out over time, making them unstable and collapsed in places. It was a priority to make the garden stock proof by rebuilding them and a delight to use stone to link the garden with its surroundings.

You'd have to be particularly observant, though, to notice something strange going on with the outcropping of stone next to the river. That first summer, when I was exploring my new sur-roundings, I sat on the river bank close by the house and drew some interesting rocks that had ivy trailing down their face. They formed an upward triangle fringed in a tangle of bramble and old hazel coppice, and I enjoyed drawing the layers in different widths of rock bands. The river bed in just this small area is level and unlike anywhere else along the valley. I thought no more of it for several years until I went to a talk about the geology of the North Pennines. The speaker described a fault line that runs north-south through Allendale, Weardale and Upper Teesdale, a notable geological feature resulting in titled rock strata. It is known as the Burtreeford Disturbance after the place in Weardale where it is visible between Burtreeford Bridge and Copthill Quarry. He said that the only other place where it can be seen is by the East Allen. It adds another layer of uniqueness to this already special place.

Stone: Softening Stonework with Planting

Drawing from these surroundings and the awareness of the qualities of stone throughout the valley, we have incorporated them into the design. As with the planting, it feels like a subtle dialogue between garden and landscape. In that first year, David when rebuilt the tumbledown garden walls, he also used heavy blocks of stone to create steps from one level to another. The front garden – the Flower Garden – he raised up by three stones' depth to calf height and along its top, I planted cottage garden plants that would spill over the edge. From Chesters Walled Garden, I had brought just two aubrietia plants. It had grown all over a retaining wall and I love its simplicity and easiness and its associations with village streets in spring. From those two plants, I broke off small rooted pieces to stuff into gaps along the top of the wall, and as the plants seeded themselves into the gravel path, I dug those up and added them. By bringing two from the walled garden, it was like the ark, rescuing two that could be used for new beginnings.

Other plants followed, also evacuees from Chesters. Persicarias are very useful as cut flowers, their fine spires spraying out of bouquets in a relaxed way. On the retaining wall, I grow the rockery or ground cover plant *Persicaria affinis*, which starts flowering in July and carries on well into the autumn, colour changing as it goes. Pale pink flowers deepen to crimson and russet so that you have a range to choose from. It makes a tough mat and is one of those plants described in catalogues as "spread indefinite" but it is easy enough to prune and dig back to shape it how you want. It flops gently over the top of the retaining wall, softening the edges and the front of the border, useful to bees and other pollinators.

To move it from Chesters, we sliced beneath its huge mat as if lifting turf, laid it on a groundsheet and rolled it up. It filled a trailer and, once at our house, we slid it off and straight into position. Laying it in its new – and thoroughly weeded – position, the persicaria quickly rooted in, voraciously covering up the once dull and scruffy area around the sunken septic tank.

I planted the dainty little lady's mantle, *Alchemilla conjuncta*, with its silver-edged leaves, often misnamed as *Alchemilla alpina*. Both plants have deeply divided leaflets, which is what makes them so attractive, but in *alpina* the leaflets are divided right to the bottom, whereas in *conjuncta* they are not. The backs of the grey-green leaves are covered in shining silver silk, the flowers are fine clusters of lime-green, and it is very hardy, down to -20. It seeds just enough into the gravel path for me to be able to use those plantlets, but does not take over in the same way as *Alchemilla mollis*.

Gardeners know what *Alchemilla mollis* can be like, but I would never want to be without it. Not only are the flowers an uplifting shade of chartreuse, they are very useful as fillers in bunches of flowers. After rain, every point on the scalloped edges of the leaves holds a tiny drop of water, with large beads of water pooling in the middle. These glassy droplets were believed to be the purest water, to be used in trying to turn base metals into gold in medieval alchemy, hence its scientific name. Herbalists considered it a magical plant and prescribed it for many ailments and for wound healing.

To make sure that lady's mantle does not self-seed and take over the flower borders, I limit it to one precise spot. That way, I can keep an eye on it! At the start of the central path, David created a gravelled rectangle, pushing it back into the retaining wall and leading to three steps. Along the bottom of its low walls, I planted lady's mantle so that it forms a cool green entrance to the Flower Garden. Frothy and vital in June, its colour is the perfect foil for the flowers above it, the purple of *Stachys macrantha* and alliums, magenta of *Geranium psilostemon*, the blue of viper's bugloss. To make sure that it doesn't set seed, I watch for the merest hint of the flowers starting to turn brown, and then I ruthlessly shear it all off down to ground level using one-handed Jakoti shears. I've seen gardens where just the flower stalks have been cut out, resulting in tired leaves that look more dusty and miserable as the summer progresses. By cutting down the whole plant, the clump looks bare for a week to ten days, but new leaves quickly grow and look spring fresh.

Into the sides of the steps, I have planted white violas, *Viola cornuta alba*, adding to the cool tones at the start of the central path. The same violas surround a stone trough that is in line with the front door and they also edge the steps that descend to the front terrace and the door. Repeating colours and themes is a way of creating rhythm and order so that the main borders can be much wilder in appearance. This stone trough I found for sale in a cobwebby barn in the Eden Valley whilst taking a group around the garden of the house. I had been looking for a stone container for that key point and knew instantly that it was the one – and it was inexpensive. It had to be stone to echo the stone steps above and below it and to fit in with the house, and each year I plant it with different summer bedding.

I look out for interesting stones that I can incorporate amongst the planting. One that I found half buried in the garden is the shape of a plump loaf of bread with a cavity in the top. Placed on the end of a retaining wall of the Flower Garden, it accumulated moss. I nestled three pale egg-shaped stones inside it, so that it looks like a bird's nest cosied in moss. Another stone with a niche in it holds the verdigris brass top of a long abandoned bedstead, something else that I found in the garden soil. Someone once sucked tobacco smoke through the bone-like sections of clay pipe, their centres now brown with earth. A tiny horseshoe now rests on our doorstep next to a heart-shaped stone found in the river.

When designing a garden, it helps one area to flow into the next if there is a sensitivity to the way in which one material meets another. This may be where grass meets gravel or paving, paving meets wall or brick meets stone. So I paid particular attention to the boundaries between one material and another. Sometimes this meant subtle changes from careful but unobtrusive planting. In that first spring, I wanted to create a sense of the garden having gently settled over the years, so I brought with me from Chesters a collection of native ferns. There were Hart's tongues, crinkly edged and waxy green; male ferns, large in size yet delicate with filigree; and the diminutive maidenhair spleenworts. These pretty little ferns had spore-sown themselves prolifically in the sand beds of the nursery cold frames and were easily lifted and transplanted. I tucked them into gaps down the side of steps at our new house and between the stones of north-facing retaining walls. I used polypody ferns, *Polypodium vulgare*, to fill an uncomfortable gap between the terrace and a dry-stone wall. The effect was immediate, softening and enhancing the garden's features.

Polypody means "many footed" and it well describes the way that this delightful fern creeps by hairy rhizomes along mossy walls and in damp, shady woodland where it grows epiphytically on trees. In the ideal conditions of the Lake District, stone walls, old quarries and roofs become thickly colonised by the emerald-green fronds of this evergreen fern. This has led to its use in city living walls where it can be mixed with other ferns in mosaic patterns in a modular irrigated system. It has lots of uses as a garden plant, and can in fact also be grown in the sun. In very dry summers, the tough and adaptable polypody ferns that ride the crest of the coping stones of our walls will shrivel to brown, the plants reviving once it rains.

Stone: Softening Stonework with Planting

Hart's tongue ferns, *Asplenium scolopendrium*, are also evergreen though, like polypodies, their leaves become unattractively brown by winter's end. At this point, I cut them to the crown to make way for the fresh green fiddles of new growth. Their undulating leathery fronds cast wavy shadows, and I planted these between the lawn and a dry-stone wall as if they had naturally arrived there. Large specimens of male fern, *Dryopteris filix-mas*, created a narrow green strip of planting along with hostas on the north side of the terrace wall.

My original plantings of Maidenhair spleenwort ferns, *Asplenium trichomanes*, have now reproduced, finding their own niches between the stones of the terrace retaining wall, where I can see them from the kitchen window. This fern gets its common name from the blackish central stalk, its species name *trichomanes* from the Greek meaning "hair of the head". The genus is named after the medieval belief that it cured ailments of the spleen, which is also reflected in its common name of spleenwort. According to the Doctrine of Signatures, the spleen-shaped sori on the back of the leaves indicated its herbal use. The English herbalist John Gerard wrote in his seventeenth century herbal that this little fern "consumeth and wasteth away the King's Evil and other hard swellings, and it maketh the haire of the head or beard to grow that is fallen and pulled off". The midribs, especially at the end of winter when many of the leaflets have fallen off, do suggest black hair.

I also soften the stonework with flowering plants. They can be used as a linking device between one area and another as I have done with the pretty white viola, *Viola cornuta* 'Alba'. Wedging small plants either side of the stone steps that lead up to the front Flower Garden, I repeat them along the edges of the terrace steps and grow them in the gravel area between the two. Keeping to such simplicity of design with these season-long white flowers creates a continuum between house and garden. They self-seed excessively so I hoe them from the gravel to prevent the effect becoming overdone.

Another abundant self-seeder is the Mexican daisy, *Erigeron karvinskianus*, also known as the National Trust daisy or Mexican fleabane. The terraces in front of and behind our house, half hidden by weeds when we first came here, had wide gaps between the paving stones, ideal for growing this prolific and charming plant. I had brought seed from Chesters, sweeping up the quantities that had dropped onto the matting in the greenhouse. This I brushed into the terrace gaps where it could be protected from the harder frosts, its roots and crowns surviving in the many mini microclimates. It took a few years to really establish but now the terrace is a froth of flowers all summer and autumn, a soft haze in shades of white, pink and red. The little daisies attract the smaller hoverflies such as *Syritta pipiens*, the thick-legged hoverfly, which is easily identified by its thickened rear legs. This important pollinator breeds in the compost and plays a useful role as biological control of vegetable pests such as lettuce aphids. Hoverflies such as *Syritta* are often used as biodiversity indicators and show the environmental health of this garden. Sitting on the terrace bench at the height of summer, Mexican daisies flowing round my feet, I can watch these nimble little hoverflies as they hang above flowers in a blur of wings.

I used to cut the mass of daisies back by hand in late autumn using my one-handed Jakoti shears. It was a long job, though like many garden jobs there was a satisfaction and peacefulness about steadily working through it. When David suggested he could run over them with the lawnmower, I hesitated before agreeing that it was worth experimenting. This brilliant idea has saved me a lot of time and with the crown of the plants and the roots still safely tucked away in the paving gaps, the plants have come to no harm. I can scoop up thick mats of germinating seeds to give to other gardeners. The paving can then be pressure washed to prevent slipping on the algae that forms under the daisy foliage.

Wood: a Ready Harvest

The valley looks the way it does because much of it is made up of two key elements: wood and stone. To unite garden and landscape, we wanted to use just these twin materials in its construction and to derive both wood and stone from the area close to the house. There is something very simple and beautiful in taking a handsaw to the woods, selecting a hazel pole and using it that same day in making arch or fence. Keeping out rabbits is an obvious must for gardeners and next to the burn was a short section where we could not build a stone wall. I decided the solution was to make tightly woven hazel hurdles that could be moved when necessary, a practical but pleasing fence when viewed from the kitchen window. Hazel is lovely wood to work with, its straight poles a soft silver-grey. Coppicing prolongs the life of a hazel tree, which can be cut down to just above ground level on an eight- to ten-year cycle. New shoots spring from the base and the resulting growth is straight, useful for bean poles and garden structures, while the topmost branches fan out and are perfect for twiggy pea sticks. This means that there's a rise and fall of the canopy over those years, with woodland flora benefiting from the increased light levels. Dormant foxglove seeds burst into life and primroses flourish.

I cut enough coppiced hazel to make three panels and, never having made hurdles before, I asked local green woodsman Saul Blenkarn to teach me how to weave the hazel. Finding a level area of the field to work on, he cut a series of upright staves known as sails. These he drove into the ground and we wove the hazel around them, twisting the thinner poles around the ends to prevent them splitting. It was hard work on the hands, especially the twisting of the hazel rods, which was necessary to break the fibres and make them pliable. We made two panels this way, the same height as the dry-stone wall that they would be butted up against. Once made, they could be pulled out of the turf and moved into position.

Saul then drove an ash pole into the field and cut slanting sides at the top to form what is known as a riving post. Using the angle of the wedge-shaped top, the hazel could be pushed against it lengthways and split right down the centre of the pole. It took a while for me to get it right but it was immensely satisfying to see the wood cleave cleanly down its length. We could then use some of the hazel entire and some split in what is known as a Westmoreland panel. The split pieces were trimmed by shaving with a double-handed drawknife whilst sitting on a wooden shavehorse. The central Westmoreland panel with its decorative contrast between split and whole hazel wands made a small gate in the fence. It was a tiring but creative day and lovely to see the western light shining through the panels with the fields beyond, a product of the valley in which the house and garden sit.

The hazel panels lasted for eight years before they were buffeted and broken by a series of powerful gales. We replaced them with willow, woven in situ onto hazel uprights. Willow easily roots when driven into the ground, hence the use of hazel sails. To prolong its life, we wait until after a prolonged spell of very dry weather and then spray the fence every year using a 50/50 mixture of pure turpentine and linseed oil. I was intrigued to notice the result of spray drift on the Solomon's seal, *Polygonatum* x *hybridum*, that grows next to fence. Compared to others in the border, this particular clump did not get ravaged by sawfly. The black flies of *Phymatocera aterrima*, on the wing in May or June, lay their eggs on the underside of the leaves. The larvae hatch like grey-white caterpillars and eat voraciously, growing fatter and fatter, and completely defoliating the Solomon's seal in a short time. It never hurts the plant, which once again the following year produces its graceful arching stems and dangling bell-shaped flowers.

Hazel was also my material of choice for creating a screen on the west end of the log shelter. We inherited the log store, which is open-sided to the south and with a sloping roof supported by old oak beams that were once in our house, and were quick to disguise the breeze block interior with split and drying logs. That first winter when we were snowed in, the drifts worked their way into the logs, wetting and making them useless for burning. Choosing straight lengths of hazel, I experimented with cleaving them lengthways using a billhook, the wood a pleasure to work. They could then be fixed to the end of the log-store, filtering the wind, preventing snow and rain getting in and looking just right. I even had fun making a hook for my spade by splitting a short length at the point where a branch stuck out.

Log burners only work efficiently if the wood is thoroughly seasoned. Prunings of hawthorn, fallen beech branches, an ash tree that had to be felled because of dieback disease, all were split on a massive roundel of log or cut up on a home-made sawhorse. As with dry-stone walling, David has eye for the Tetris-like fitting together of shapes and the log store is a thing of beauty. In order to keep wood of different ages in separate sections, he builds freestanding stacks beneath the cover by using logs placed on the corners at 90 degrees, effectively as quoins. This means that we can take out the oldest, most seasoned wood whilst the rest dries out.

Coppiced hazel also makes sturdy bean poles, straight enough to be practical but irregular enough to look right. Their slightly rough surface allows runner beans to get a hold as they twine their way up. If you buy hazel bean poles instead of bamboo canes, you are helping to support the coppicing of woodland with all its wildlife benefits and carbon storage. At the end of each season, we lift the poles from the ground, clean the mud from the base and store them in the dry so that they last for several years. I also noticed a mass of silver birch that had been felled just a mile away and re-grown tall and straight after a few years. Getting permission to cut this, we harvested large bundles to use in the Vegetable Garden. Pea supports were made using poles at intervals, strengthened by cross poles and with a lattice of twiggy prunings from the hardy fuchsias as a tracery for the peas to scramble up.

The willow spiling on the riverbank two fields away was a source of material for making wigwams for sweet peas and other climbing annuals. Poking a ring of twelve willow wands into the ground, I wove between them with more of the long and flexible shoots, creating a series of diminishing circles towards the top. Binding the crown tightly with tarred twine, I trimmed the wands to the same height; the result was a willow obelisk made in a couple of hours and costing nothing. The willow generally roots itself but is easy enough to take out at the end of a season. It is also useful for making supports for herbaceous plants such as peonies by twisting together a couple of willow wands to form a circular frame. Four pieces of willow can then be inserted into it in the pattern of a noughts and crosses board, the whole then held horizontal by threading it and tying onto four uprights above the crown of the emerging plant.

A number of craftsmen work with wood in the Allen Valleys. A few miles away is the Burnlaw Centre, a small loose-knit community informed by Baha'i, Buddhist, environmental and co-operative thinking. At the centre of its forty acres of organic pastures, woodland and gardens is a hamlet of stone-built houses, the oldest a bastle house. Several creative businesses are based here, with activities such as filmmaking, green woodworking and painting. The Canvas Awning Company make woodsman's awnings using poles made of coppiced ash and thicket larch from locally sourced woodlands that are topped with a cover of thick canvas. Logs are stored to dry at Burnlaw using the German system of *Holzhausen*, circular stacks of drying timber topped in sloping roofs of wood or bark and looking like small round buildings.

Jonah Maurice lives off-grid on a fourteen-acre smallholding in a wooden house that he built himself, all the timber sourced from directly around his home in Allendale. As a woodsman, he often has to work on steeply sloping terrain, sometimes using horse power to haul timber from difficult or easily damaged areas. As a carpenter, he gets inspiration from how the wood suggests itself, as in the quirky shelter he built for Allendale's community garden project Higher Ground. Topped by a swept-up shingle roof, the main supports are squashed curves taken from splitting a wonky tree trunk into two halves. The result, with its hint of Russian, Indian or fairytale, is delightfully weird.

The woodlands from which these craftsmen harvest timber benefit from active management. Without this, they become dark and dominated by the thick canopy of mature trees but without the different levels of understory that provide for mixed wildlife habitat. Felling on rotation, coppicing and leaving a combination of open glades and cover makes for a variety of conditions. Leaving piles of wood to rot down is valuable for mosses, ferns, lichen and fungi, and makes a place for beetles, insects, frogs, toads, newts and slow worms. In a quiet corner of our garden, I used short upright hazel posts interwoven with willow as a frame for piles of prunings, leaves and grass stalks. After reading about *Hugelkultur*, I began experimenting with decaying logs in the base of large containers for growing.

Hugelkultur has been used for many years in Eastern Europe and in Germany. It's a type of raised bed system – the word translates as "mound culture" – that uses the gradual decay of wood to power the heap, providing the nutrients needed for plants to thrive.

Steep-sided long raised beds are started with brush wood, logs and branches before being covered in turf laid face-downwards with soil on top. The rotting wood releases heat just as in a compost heap; it acts as a sponge to store rainwater and it feeds the plants.

Wanting to plant up a three-foot-high galvanised water tank by the back door, I realised it was going to need a large volume of compost and this method of permaculture offered a solution. I laid the bottom third with logs that had begun to decay before covering them with smaller branches and was able to use a relatively small amount of compost on top. With the tank facing east and being in semi shade, the kind of woodland plants that I filled it were ideal for this system: *Epimedium* 'Amber Queen', *Hakonechloa macra* 'Aureola', the variegated form of Japanese forest grass, and fritillaries. In three years, the plants in the container have not needed to be fed and even during drought conditions they need very little water.

Following that success, I used *Hugelkultur* in a wooden-sided raised bed in which to grow herbs for cooking. In the working area and near to the back door, it's surrounded by woodchip so that we can pick without getting muddy feet. The base of the bed I lined with branches that had started to decay followed by twiggy material, all then topped in soil from the Vegetable Garden. Along with a useful mixture of bushy thymes, chives, coriander and parsley, I've risked some French tarragon, a plant that usually needs to be grown in a greenhouse in our area. It's a division of the main plant that has been in the soil of the greenhouse now for nearly twelve years, and when frosts are forecast I have put an upturned pot over it but no fleece. It has surprisingly survived, maybe thanks to the warming effect of *Hugelkultur's* base of rotting wood. All around us in the woodland, the process of growth and decay forms a cycle. My small raised herb bed uses that process and is a microcosm of what is happening out there in the woods.

Learning from Landscape:
Creating Habitat Layers
in the Garden

It is through looking at the landscape around that we learn what to do in our garden and how to make it a rich place for wildlife. Key to this is the creation of layers of planting. I think of it a series of horizontal bands of growth from diminutive alpines through ascending levels of perennials to shrubs and trees. Making a wildlife garden is about forming as diverse a range of habitats as possible. Ours is a scaled-down version of the matrix that exists outside our boundary walls, of water, grassland, trees and scrub. It's a multi-layered approach of niches and places for each type of wildlife.

The first layer is the soil, which is why that was our priority when we first moved here. Reinvigorating the compacted damaged earth with homemade compost and avoiding walking on it led to it being quickly filled with earthworms, beetles, woodlice, mites, millipedes, nematodes and thousands of soil animals to break down rotting plants and to be food for birds. It has become easy to work, an ecosystem that is alive once more. The organic mulches that we apply every year break down to encourage wide-ranging soil organisms, and if we now have slugs and snails where there were few before, these are eaten by thrushes and blackbirds. No one insect expands to pest proportions because there is always something to predate on it and thrive. The garden has settled into balance.

The inorganic mulches of gravel also provide homes for wildlife. Whorled strawberry snails with fragile shells are no bigger than the stones that make up the gravel. Woodlice congregate beneath terracotta pots, scuttling for darkness and safety when disturbed. Spiders run across the paved terraces, disappearing back down into the gaps, and there are frequently stoneflies that have emerged from the river. Tiny black-and-white-striped zebra spiders leap to catch their prey from walls and sun-warmed doors. As the gravel heats during the day, it becomes a surface for butterflies to sunbathe. The alpine plants growing in the gravel are snug places for ladybirds, mossy saxifrages create dense mats. Ground cover such as persicaria and *Geranium* 'St Ola' is low-lying and thickly carpeting; raise a corner of it and it's busy with small life forms living beneath its roof.

Patches of bare ground are suitable for solitary bees to make their nests. Chocolate mining bees, *Andrena scotica*, make their homes in the dry soil in front of our compost bins. These are solitary bees, the females laying eggs in separate burrows but sharing a common entrance hole. Each egg will hatch into a larva, eat the stored pollen and pupate before emerging as an adult. I love to watch the females flying in with their full pollen baskets to store the food that their young will feed on in their individual chambers. They also nest at the bottom of the low retaining that drops down from the front garden on to the terrace where I can sit on a bench and watch them.

Amongst the low growing plants are the spring bulbs that give early nectar for bees in the form of snowdrops and snowflakes. There are little blue scillas and chinodaxas, white Ipheion, cups of crocus and grape hyacinths. Daffodils are planted across the garden, the later emergence of perennials hiding their foliage as it yellows and feeds back into the bulbs. Tulips look sumptuous in containers by the door and the old cottage garden favourite 'Apeldoorn' comes up reliably every year in brilliant red alongside the main cross path. Bumblebees nose up inside the dusky hanging bells of snakes' head fritillaries. The frits are happy in the damp soil and seed themselves into the spreading mats of lungwort where dark-edged bee flies, *Bombylius major*, hover to suck nectar through extended probosces. After the first flowering of the shorter plants such as cowslip, bugle and thrift, there's a free-for-all of honesty, which I allow to grow right through the borders, a favourite, along with Jack-by-the-hedge, of orange-tip butterflies.

The next level is of hummocky plants with mounds of basal growth, clump-forming plants and grasses. As I cut the whitened leaves from the Algerian iris, seared by biting easterlies in winter, there's the musty smell of mice and voles where its thick cover has been a cold season nesting place. Beneath the thatch of *Stipa gigantea* is where hedgehogs hibernate. Tussocky grasses make safe hideaways from predators, and have a warm microclimate. Leaving long grass around the lawn gives a variation in sward height for ground beetles and bumblebees, and food plants for moth and butterfly caterpillars.

As the Flower Garden grows from spring onwards it rises and falls in wave-like rhythms with plants at different heights. Keeping it weed-free early on – I aim to have all weeded and mulched by late April – I can leave it virtually undisturbed. In a knee-high thicket of white oriental comfrey a garden warbler weaves a cup-shaped nest of pale straw, lined with darker fine roots and hair. In late summer, mothercare spiders, *Theridion sisyphium*, anchor their nests between the sturdy tops of the sea hollies. Inside a spun chamber are blue egg sacs studded with insect food: bits of bluebottle flies or a wasp. From the sac will emerge a mass of tiny spiderlings with pale olive legs and little round bodies. The spider feeds her young on regurgitated food until they are large enough to share her meals and when she dies, they will eat her body.

The mass of – mostly single – flowers is made up of a huge

variety of plant shapes, each suitable for different insects. Flowers are made of tubes, bells, are flat-topped or open-cupped, tiny or expansive, discreet or flamboyant. It's the diversity that matters, both on the eye and for the insect life they support. Over the years, I've observed which flowers are most popular in this mid layer. The shaggy yellow daisies of *Inula hookeri* for butterflies, the sky-blue funnel shaped flowers of Viper's bugloss for bees, the spreading mounds of *Nepeta* 'Six Hills Giant', reliable, long-flowering. It provides such a mass of food all in one place that bees can conserve their energy by not having to fly to other nectar sources. Spires of silvery lambs' ears, *Stachys byzantina*, feed bumblebees, their felted leaves being combed of their hairs by wool carder bees, *Anthidium manicatum*, to line their nests.

Some flower structures are easier for insects to access, in particular daisies and umbels. They are both made up of many tiny individual flowers all brought together in one composite flower head and providing a wealth of pollen and nectar in one place. Daisies, such as the ox-eye of the meadow, have yellow disc florets at their centres with white petal-like ray-florets arranged around the edge as in a child's imagined flower. From the common daisies in our lawn to the annual cosmos and the perennial heleniums and echinacea, there's a huge range of daisy flower colours and sizes to attract insects.

Umbellifers are the cow parsley family. Some form round globes such as Angelica, whilst others have flattened tops like small parasols or umbrellas. They have many small flowers attached by spokes to a central point and hollow stems where insects can overwinter. In growing a range of umbellifers and loving their billowy lightness, I draw on memories of growing up in a landscape of small lanes lined with frothy cow parsley at May blossom time. An image of a certain moment in the year, as in a painting by David Hockney. Apart from the purple *Anthriscus* 'Raven's Wing'

Creating Habitat Layers in the Garden

and a few plants of the species that are allowed (and deadheaded or they would take over), it is the more refined alternatives to cow parsley that make it into the borders.

There's *Ammi majus* and *Ammi visnaga*, grown from seed each year, and *Orlaya grandiflora*, known as white lace flower, its small inner flowers edged with large outer florets and looking like a lace-cap hydrangea. The snowy-white flowers dance above ferny foliage and echo the smaller native pignut that I grow amongst the thyme. In the Vegetable Garden, I let some of the herbs and veg go to seed, partly for the loose cow parsley-like effect, partly for the benefit to insects. Stately fennel, feathery dill, emerald-green parsley and delicate coriander all have flat open flowers and a relaxed wildflower effect. As well as many of our best vegetables and herbs, the family includes poisonous plants such as musty-smelling hemlock as well as parsnips, whose leafy tops can cause painful blistering, particularly in sunny conditions. Umbellifers have become very popular amongst designers at garden shows because they have such interesting structure. They help provide that link to the landscape and the wild, partly visually and partly for the benefit of wildlife.

Above the mid-height layer of perennials, of flat-topped achilleas, hardy geraniums and autumn sedum abundance, the tallest plants rise up throughout the growing season. In the open courtyard of the terrace, there are hollyhocks, their backs to a dry-stone wall, their petals flung wide open for foraging bees. Growing at this tallest level of perennials, there's the huge angelicas, the ebullient pink meadowsweet, towering grass seedheads and clouds of milky bellflower. The autumn culmination is of plants that grow way above my head, reminiscent of that feeling as a child when I would look up at the numerous butterflies on purple asters and try and take photographs on an Instamatic camera. Joe Pye Weed, *Eupatorium purpureum*, normally grows to seven or eight feet tall, and is much loved by insects. This tall pink-purple scented flower is named after an Indian healer from New England who used the plant for a variety of ailments including kidney stones and fevers.

Joe Pye Weed eventually makes a rock-hard root system. Moving it from Chesters was challenging, especially as my energy levels were flagging. It had filled out to an eight-foot-square mass, and it was a kind friend who chopped it into manageable two-foot-square portions with a heavy and sharp spade so that we could put them into crates ready for transporting. You can tell what kind of season we are having from the height of the Joe Pye. It needs a moisture-retentive soil and dry summers can result in it being two or three feet shorter than in a wetter year. It's one of my favourite choices for autumn flower bunches.

The Joe Pye Weed was already in the garden at Chesters when I took it over, along with a few other intriguing plants such as birthwort, *Aristolochia clematitis*. I wondered if they had been there purely for decorative reasons or perhaps as medicinal plants on the estate, maybe for veterinary use. Now when I look across the Flower Garden, I know exactly where plants grew in the borders of the walled garden, and they are overlaid with these memories. They behave differently in different soils; the acanthus that was so invasive at Chesters is here more modest in its range, the white rosebay willowherb that barely expanded from its dry position, here needs yearly restricting of its vigorous roots. Their combinations are new too, like making a different recipe from the same ingredients.

Next in the horizontal layers of planting comes the shrubs. In early spring, the pink dangling blooms of flowering redcurrant attract bees in the woodland border. At the back of this border, and beneath the spreading canopy of the sycamores, I've planted four native junipers to echo the wild junipers that grow in the valley. Near them are the tall knobbly branches of tree peonies, yellow and deep red flowered, the shade beneath their feet enlivened by the lime-green tops of perfoliate alexanders. That corkscrew hazel, the first shrub planted and a survivor of the move from Chesters, provides safety and a stopping off point for a range of small birds. The pair of amelanchiers, focal point at the end of the path from the front door, flower in late April if not too many of their buds are taken by bullfinches.

I can see just how many birds use the pair of *Eleagnus* 'Quicksilver' that grow along the cross path by the number of seedlings found beneath them. Deposited seed from the berries of hawthorn, bird cherry and roses sprout into a ring of young plants beneath these silver shrubs. Wrens enjoy the density of the yew topiary and I have to be careful when clipping it to check first if wasps have built their nests in the dark interior. Buddleias ring the terrace so that we have their sweet scent when sitting in this warm enclosed area. Famous as the butterfly bush, there can be several different species of butterfly at once crowding its long purple racemes. The two old viburnums with their thicket of interlacing branches house several different species of birds' nests.

In the smaller trees, pigeons and blackbirds nest in the hawthorns and bird cherries. Long-tailed tits swing like acrobats along the branch ends, delicately picking off aphids. The final layer in this multi-layered sandwich of wildlife niches is the mature trees, the sycamore and ash. Greater spotted woodpeckers work their way over trunk and branches, tap-tapping or flying off with an alarm call if I'm outside. If they know they've been seen, they slip round the far side of the tree trunk, head peeping round like a child playing a game. By night, tawny owls call from the trees and bats fly up and down the line of trees after insects. Beneath the bark live millipedes and woodlice, earwigs and spiders, whilst several species of moth caterpillar eat the leaves. Sycamores attract aphids, which in turn bring in ladybirds, lacewings and birds. The trees are the top level in this ecological lasagne of different habitats.

This all links to the world outside the garden, to the woods, the rough pasture and scrub. Of this mass of garden plants, the alpines, low-growing and ground coverers, are the height of the plants of the woodland floor, the wild garlic, bluebells and primroses in the surrounding landscape. The layer above that is like the understory of waist-height bramble and bilberry. Higher than that are the garden shrubs that emulate the scrub layer of gorse and broom. Then there are the trees that edge the woodland border and form a summer canopy of shade. There's an echoing of forms too in the upward sweep of the branches of *Eleagnus* 'Quicksilver' that relates to the similar shape of the ash trees, of the viburnum clipped into the rounded form of the skyline sycamore.

In aiming to provide shelter, home and food for all the various forms of wildlife, I've tried to make a mixture of the patterns of growth that I see in the wider landscape. To leave areas undisturbed and borders thick enough to provide cover. To learn from the landscape in the way that I garden. Yet it is organised and has to work visually too. I passionately believe that a wildlife garden does not have to be an untidy garden and I want to be able to look out from the house and see beauty and order as well. The garden does not impose but is a response to the North Pennine landscape and is inspired by it.

Meadow

If the exuberant Flower Garden draws inspiration from the North Pennine uplands, I wanted there to be a place as well for something more modest, something more similar to its celebrated hay meadows. This evolved naturally from allowing free rein to the grasses around the lawn in a metre-wide strip. The lawn itself is full of wildflowers such as clover, daisy and speedwell, giving food to insects. It is not cut too short so that they can bloom, but short enough to be able to comfortably throw down a rug and gaze up at the swallows criss-crossing the sky. The meadow strips gave existing wildflowers the opportunity to grow to their full height. In the corner where the ugly barbecue had been – what a joy it was to demolish it – there was good drainage from the stony ground beneath the turf. I had brought with me from Chesters a box of orchids growing in short grass, a treasured gift from a Tyne Valley garden where they had been found in a lawn. Common spotted orchids, *Dactylorhiza fuchsii*, they thrive on a symbiotic relationship with a fungus that is necessary for them to germinate and grow. This is why I had kept them in their box of turf for all those years, waiting for a suitable garden in which to release them. The small well-drained triangle where the barbecue had been was just right for a miniature meadow.

As well as the wild strips around the lawn and the meadow triangle, a wide grassy sweep leads to the river gate. This we also allowed to grow out, with just a mown path in a curve down the middle. After a couple of seasons, the wildflowers that had been repressed through lawn cutting were able to flourish. Crosswort, *Cruciata laevipes*, has tiny yellow flowers smelling of honey all spring and summer, its four leaves arranged around the stem to form a cross, giving it its common name. The general impression is of lime green, the same colour as lady's mantle, as if sunlight has fallen across the plant. Knapweed or hardheads, *Centaurea nigra*, can over dominate a meadow, but its nectar attracts butterflies bees and beetles, its seeds give food for birds. Purple thistle flowers open in late season when other meadow plants have gone to seed. I just have to make sure that it doesn't crowd out other flowers. These UK natives grew spontaneously once we let the grass go long, added to by wood avens, germander speedwell, primrose and plantain.

Into these meadow areas I introduced plants that I had brought with me or that I grew from seed. Into the damper place near the river went ragged robin, *Silene flos-cuculi*, named for the "flower of the cuckoo" because of its timing. It has fringed pink petals that look like they have been buffeted and torn by the wind, and is related to red campion, *Silene dioica*, which I also planted into the meadow. Both these wild plants seed themselves freely and I also let them grow through the semi-shaded border in front of the house. Red Campion grows strongly and can be a bit over-dominant so I will edit out some of the plants, but ragged robin with its finer leaves is a delight when it pops up in unexpected places. Growing wildflowers and allowing lots of self-seeding does require some curating but seedlings can be moved into the long grass and meadow areas.

In 2004, I described a year in the life of a small hay meadow for a concertina booklet commissioned as part of The Haytime Project by the North Pennines National Landscape. Inspired by a local meadow, it was a collaboration with artist Kim Lewis, whose series of country picture books for children are world-wide classics. My children grew up reading *Floss*, *Emma's Lamb* and other tales of farming and shepherding life. Kim's light-filled drawings and engravings of wildflowers and grasses accompanied my lyrical essay and homage to this special place.

Meadow

It was to this meadow that I went one August just before the tractor and baler arrived and collected a small paper bag of the seeds of yellow rattle, *Rhinanthus minor*. This annual wildflower is semi-parasitic on grasses, drawing water and nutrients from them and suppressing their vigour by as much as 60 per cent. By stunting the growth of the grasses, yellow rattle gives other wildflowers room to grow and is an essential ingredient in making a species-rich meadow. Once its yellow flowers fade, having been pollinated by bumblebees, the pods of rattle inflate to hold the seed. Once dry, they can be shaken like tiny maracas, a signal to farmers that it is time to cut the hay. Yellow rattle seed is only viable for a year so if the hay crop is cut too early, there's no previous year's progeny left to germinate.

Yellow rattle needs to be sown as fresh as possible. I took that initial handful back to my miniature meadow and, after scratching amongst the turf with a rake to expose the soil, I pressed the seed into the surface much as the hooves of animals would do. Some months of winter cold are necessary for germination, which is why this needs to be done at the latest by November so that frost can break the seeds' dormancy. The next spring, up popped the little seedlings, and that summer they flowered and set their own seed. This one small handful of yellow rattle from my neighbour's field has multiplied year on year, helped by my collecting my own pods and shaking them into new areas of grass. Where the rattle is thickest, the grasses are noticeably shorter, allowing the orchids to increase and for cranesbills, eyebright and cowslips to thrive with less competition. My patch of orchids has grown from a handful to twenty-nine, and I count them every year.

Mine is a perennial meadow, managed much as local farmers do the hay, and not to be confused with an annual meadow. The latter is brightly coloured with blue cornflowers, scarlet field poppies, purple corncockle and yellow corn marigolds; many people's idealised concept of a meadow. These are all annual plants that need yearly sowing and the mix doesn't include the grasses that would dilute the effect. The preparation for annuals is straightforward and involves clearing the ground completely of weeds and raking the seedbed to a fine tilth. It should be sown in spring, ideally just before light rain, making sure there is good contact between the seed and the soil and protecting it from birds.

Poppy seed germinates when it is brought to the surface, triggered by exposure to light. That is why poppies bloomed *en masse* on the churned up battlefields of northern France after the First World War and why they can be seen in summer cornfields, especially those ploughed in spring when the seed is freshly uncovered. The lines and swathes of red often indicate the depth to which the plough has been worked. Field poppies, *Papaver rhoeas*, have one of the longest dormancies of British wildflowers, capable of waiting in the soil for many decades until the right moment when they are brought to the surface. Poppies and other cornfield annuals cannot survive in the sward of a perennial meadow because they are denied the light. The traditional hay meadow is less showy but is self-sustaining once it is established and has a more subtle charm. Both types can be scaled down to fit into modern small gardens and I've seen successful and colourful annual meadows in front of terraced houses. The size of my perennial meadow triangle is far smaller than many front gardens.

My own tiny patch of grass and wildflowers shows just what can be done. As well as those precious orchids, the ox-eye daisies are flourishing. Also known as moon daisy, *Leucanthemum vulgare* blooms for a long period and produces a mass of seed. It's a pioneer species of grassland and can be dominant in a newly sown meadow. Whole banks of ox-eye daisies spread alongside motorways or beside railway lines.

Meadow

After this froth of white comes yellow in the form of St John's Wort. This valuable healing herb, *Hypericum perforatum*, has, as its species name indicates, what appear to be small perforations in its leaves that are visible when it is held up to the light. They are actually translucent resin glands that give off a scent that is sometimes described as "foxy". Look closely at St John's Wort's yellow petals and you will see black steaks and dots. Crush the petals, or especially the flower bud, between your fingers and they will be stained purple-red. If the flowers are infused in olive oil and left in sunshine, it will turn a rich purple in a few days. Applied to the skin, it is used for sunburn and in cosmetics. St John's Wort has a long history of herbal use, with a lot of recent interest in its properties in particular for the treatment of depression. In clinical trials, about 67 per cent of patients with mild to moderate depression improved when taking this plant, but it should be used with caution and only on medical advice. For dyers and weavers, various colours can be obtained from the flowers or leaves giving red, yellow, gold or brown, depending on how and from what part of the plant they are extracted.

Having run a herb garden for twenty-three years, I've retained a fascination with the properties and stories of plants. In the shade of the toolshed wall, I planted woodruff, a delightful native plant. With its ruff of green leaves arranged in whorls up the stem, woodruff, *Galium odoratum*, is a dainty perennial with starry white flowers in spring. When picked, the plant gives off a scent of new mown hay because of the coumarin in its leaves. If you separate a ruff of leaves, detaching it from the stem above and below, it can be flattened to form a shape like a rose-window in a cathedral. This was traditionally pressed into books and bibles as a page marker, the smell of hay lingering for years.

Woodruff is a joyful plant with its spring green leaves, white starry flowers and comforting scent. By soaking it in white wine, it is made into a fresh tasting punch in Germany where it is known as "*Maibowle*" because of its flowering time. Woodruff grows in the semi-ancient woodlands of the valley, an indicator of their age along with others such as dog's mercury and wild garlic. I unintentionally introduced it to the woodland border where it had hitched a ride in some variegated irises from Chesters. It rapidly expanded at a time when I had too much else to do to control it and it has run extensively in the border. With its small size and natural summer die-back as the leaf canopy expands, it doesn't seem to crowd out other plants, but it is a reminder that this can be an invasive plant in the good soil of a garden.

In my meadow and in the shade of the shed wall it spreads less, the conditions being more like its native habitat. Alongside it is another UK plant, wood sage, *Teucrium scorodonia*, which has crinkled, lightly scented leaves and greenish-yellow flowers. It's a woodland edge plant, one that I find growing, sometimes in abundance, on dry banksides below the heather moors. A rather discreet plant, it can be overlooked, but it flowers over a long period and is pollinated by bees.

Much more showy is melancholy thistle, the same that I am growing in the Flower Garden, but here in the more usual combination with grasses. In that blurring of the boundaries between the wild and the cultivated, I have introduced some garden plants into the meadow – thalictrum with its delicate bobbing purple flowers, cultivars of hardy geraniums such as 'Amy Doncaster', lupins, aquilegias and camassias. They add to the colour mix with native red clover, vetch, scabious and meadowsweet, *Filipendula ulmaria*. Also known as Queen of the meadow, this thrives in damp places, often becoming the dominant plant. I have watched it spread across a local north-facing hillside over the past fourteen years, where it has revelled in the damp soil and crowded out other species. The fragrance of its flowers hits you as you emerge from the wood into the light of the valley, a combination of sweetness with a slightly bitter undertone of almond. Flowers and leaves smell very different, giving rise to the old name of "courtship and matrimony", the sweet flowers representing courtship, the bitter leaves the reality of marriage. It's from the salicin in these leaves, which smell antiseptically like TCP, that in 1897 Felix Hoffmann created a pure and stable form of acetylsalicylic acid and it was named aspirin after its old botanical name of *Spiraea*. As with the knapweed, I manage the meadowsweet so that it does not take over.

Early August is hay time in the North Pennines. As I work in the garden, I can smell hay, the scent drifting down on a light breeze from the fields above the valley. A settled forecast is the trigger as farm after farm gets busy with the haymaking that ripples in a wave across the surrounding hills. This is when I too cut down the grasses and wildflowers that have brought such a loose, free feeling in contrast to the shorter sward of the lawn. We take care to remove all the hay in order to keep the soil fertility low, which is necessary for the growth of wildflowers rather than hungry feeders such as docks and nettles. Going over it again with a wire rake gets up any last bits of debris, all good for the compost heap, and exposes small bare patches into which the displaced seeds can tumble. To imitate the winter grazing of livestock, we will go over it with the mower a few times before spring. The orchids set their seed later than the rest of the meadow so I stake their position with canes and work around them. Orchid seed is dust-fine and it takes seven years for orchids to mature and flower. To give them the best chance, I wait til the pods are completely ripe before shaking them low to the ground into exposed soil, hoping to increase them in future years. Like much gardening, it is about thinking ahead and being patient.

In winter, this area looks much like the lawn. On a dreich January day, I look at it and imagine summer when bumblebees are noisy in the flowers of vetch and knapweed. Ox-eye daisies sway on tall stems and there are flashes of vivid pink from ragged robin and softer pink of orchids. I glimpse the tail of a slow worm as it disappears between the grasses. Swallows chatter constantly as they fly overhead scooping up insects and buzzards make slow mewing circles against the sky. As with the Flower Garden, it is the rise and fall of the meadow and the seasonal contrasts that make it feel so alive.

Wildflowers in Borders

Throughout history, there has been a two-way movement between gardens and landscape. Plants have escaped from gardens to become permanently established outside their walls. Wild plants with attractive flowers or herbal uses have been brought into our gardens. Naturally occurring variants of native plants – those with double flowers or unusual colouring – have been treasured and nurtured. This blurring of definition between the wild and the cultivated is something that I joyfully embrace and it fits in with the naturalistic style in which I garden.

This has not been particularly conscious. I just plant what I like. But when I came to make a list of the native plants that are mingled into the borders of the Flower Garden, I was astonished to find that they numbered seventy. If I include the coloured forms of wild plants – such as white rosebay willowherb – then that increases to eighty-two. Some have just appeared thanks to the setting, wildlings that were present as dormant seed in the soil and that germinated because of being brought to the surface by moles. Long ago, the garden would have been farmland, so these are meadow species such as pignut.

I first noticed some pignut, *Conopodium majus*, rising out of a spreading carpet of thyme. This delicate white-flowered umbellifer is a summer feature of the old hay meadows of the North Pennines and the caterpillar food plant for the chimney sweeper moth, *Odezia atrata*. These delightful, small sooty black moths have white edges to their forewings. They fly by day, especially when it is sunny. The meadows near our house are sprinkled with a soft white fuzz when the pignut is in flower, the moths skipping fast between them on fluttering wings. Their tiny green larvae eat the flowers and seeds of pignut. As a forage plant for rootling pigs, it is the knobbly tubers of this low growing umbellifer that give the plant its name. When my children were young, I taught them how to dig deep in the soil to find the little edible tubers that taste like peppery hazelnuts. Once the plant has flowered and gone to seed, the basal leaves wither and the whole thing is easily overlooked. It's because it casts so little shade and doesn't impact on other plants that I have been able to let pignut seed itself throughout the wide bands of thyme that border the path to the greenhouse. It's a diminutive echo of the popular *Ammi majus* that is so often seen in gardens at the Chelsea Flower Show.

Providing food plants for moth and butterfly caterpillars is often overlooked whilst gardeners focus on plants for pollinators to feed from in their more visible adult stages. These colourful flying insects get all the attention but without food for their larvae, they wouldn't be on the wing. Better publicity is usually given to food for butterfly caterpillars: nettles for red admiral, peacock, comma and small tortoiseshell, or Jack by the hedge and lady's smock for orange-tip butterflies and green-veined whites. There are fifty-seven resident species of butterflies in the UK but over 2,500 species of moths, each needing not only nectar-bearing flowers for adults but the right food plants for their larval stages. The greater the variety of plants that we include in our gardens, the more we can support them, especially as some moth caterpillars will only eat one type of plant. Native plants, especially those that are found in the North Pennines, are most likely to benefit the moth species that are already present in our valley. Dandelion is the food plant for the orange swift moth, juniper for mottled beauty, primrose for silver-ground carpet and yellow flag iris for red sword-grass.

Wildflowers in Borders

Blending wildflowers into the garden is something that I have done instinctively. These are nomad plants, always on the move, settling where they feel is right. Some are given free rein, others have to be deadheaded before they can over-seed and become over-abundant. But out of all of them, cowslips are allowed to seed themselves wherever they like and I rarely move them, only if they are in a path and likely to be trodden on or making it difficult to hoe. Then they are popped into a border. The primulas – cowslips, primroses and oxlips – bloom before the borders have filled out, delightful sunshine pools of pale yellow and vibrant fresh leaves. The seeds of primroses are distributed by ants who are attracted by fleshy bumps on the surface of the seeds called elaisomes. These are rich in nutrients and ants carry them back to their colony to feed to their larvae. Once the elaisome has been eaten, the ants dump the seed in a waste area outside their nest; here, they can then germinate away from the original plant. As primulas set seed and their leaves diminish, they become shaded by other plants, creating the cool conditions that they like. It's the same with other wildflowers. Snakes' head fritillaries, beautiful chequered hanging bells of purple or white, are growing happily in the damp open ground of the garden in spring but are protected from too much heat later on by the mass of growth that is the Flower Garden at its fullest.

Wood anemone grows in dappled shade, flowering early in the year before the leaf canopy grows dense, a plant of ancient woodlands where its spread is slow. Seed is generally infertile so wood anemones rely on gradual colonising by their roots. It's possible to replicate these conditions in a border that has no trees or shrubs such as the meadow-like Flower Garden and each year, after the wood anemones have flowered, I split off some of the twiggy little rhizomes to move them into new spots. There, tucked safely beneath the tall stems of asters or heleniums or inulas, their leaves can shrivel, their rhizomes kept damp and cool.

There's something very simple and beautiful about the native wood anemone, *Anemone nemorosa*. Anemone derives from the Greek and means "daughter of the wind" and these nodding star-shaped flowers are also called windflower. Pollinated by hoverflies, their petals can be flushed purple or lilac on the reverse, these quirks giving rise to forms that, once discovered, have been introduced to gardens. The tall variety 'Robinsoniana' was named after William Robinson who found it growing in Oxford Botanic Garden in the late nineteenth century, though it had possibly originated from woods in Ireland. It was a favourite of his – he wrote the influential *The Wild Garden* – and by 1900 was grown in many English gardens, valued for its lavender-blue colouring. I revel in the odd flowers of native plants, so as well as growing the species, I find space for the weird green 'Virescens', its flowers made up of a mass of fine green leaves, and for the bright and serene double wood anemones such as 'Vestal'. I plant them on a raised bed amongst my favourite spring treasures where they can be really appreciated. The non-native *Anemone ranunculoides* known as wood ginger is a favourite of mine, its plentiful buttercup-yellow flowers cheering in a brisk March wind. Like our native anemones, it is summer dormant, making it ideal to grow under trees and shrubs.

Although the majority of plants in this garden are chosen for the nectar and pollen that they provide for insects – and are therefore single-flowered – I've a fondness for old-fashioned doubles and other oddities. There's the green rose plantain, *Plantago major* 'Rosularis', known since medieval times when quirky plants were particularly delighted in. The emerald-green roses are formed from a whorl of spoon-shaped bracts; it has mutated from the wild plant into something curious and rather lovely.

Wildflowers in Borders

Other wildlings that I grow have evolved more simply with different coloured flowers or leaves to the species: purple-leaved plantain, golden creeping Jenny, white water avens, white herb Robert and the bronze-leaved lesser celandine with the saucy name of 'Brazen Hussy'. The purple cow parsley, *Anthriscus sylvestris* 'Raven's Wing', was found in an Oxfordshire lane by Northumberland botanist Prof John Richards when he was leading a group looking at dandelions. He is an expert in *Taraxacum* or dandelion, a highly knowledgeable plantsman, and I was lucky to be part of a memorable Alpine Garden Society trip to Crete that he led on a particularly flower-filled spring. When John spotted a newly emerged cow parsley with deep purple foliage in that Berkshire lane, he named it 'Raven's Wing'. It is now a favourite with designers at the Chelsea Flower Show and grown worldwide.

Most of the wildflowers that I grow though are the species and they seed themselves freely amongst the cultivated plants. Red campion, *Silene dioica*, drops quantities of seed so I collect the seed pods for giving to other gardeners, and every other year I reduce its numbers. Ragged robin, *Lychnis flos-cuculi,* though is a much gentler plant, its basal leaves and delicately fringed flowers slotting in more easily between established plants. Sweet rocket came originally from a Northumberland riverbank. Wild carrot is invaluable for insects, viper's bugloss and foxgloves for bumblebees, yarrow for lacewings and beetles, greater burnet for hoverflies.

One plant I do regret giving room to is coralroot, *Cardamine bulbifera*. This pretty relative of lady's smock spreads not only by its knobbly rootstock but by the bulbils that sit in the axils of its flowering stems. It is easy to knock these off when working in a border and helping it to work its way throughout. Although it is useful in that it will grow in dry shade, I find it very invasive, which makes it surprising that it is a rare British plant in the wild.

Second Nature

Sanicle too is making itself a bit too much at home in my woodland border so I now go through and deadhead it after flowering, collecting its prickly little seeds. I like to grow this since it is a plant that grows wild in the valley and is an indicator of ancient woodland. It's one of those rather unusual historic herbs that I brought with me from Chesters. There, I grew it as an example of an all-round herbal remedy, once taken for wound healing, blood disorders, chest complaints and sore throats, though it is little used today because of the potentially harmful compounds it contains. It is, though, a pretty and dainty umbellifer, its glossy green leaves attractively shaped and sculpted, and I like the link between what I am growing in my garden and what has grown for centuries in the surrounding woods.

Local meadows glow with buttercups in spring, with whole fields golden yellow from a distance. Gardeners know how buttercups, especially creeping buttercup, can easily take over, but for many years I have grown a well-behaved variety that I used to sell in the nursery at Chesters. The woolly buttercup, *Ranunculus lanuginosus*, comes from central and eastern Europe so it is not native to the UK but it creates the same effect without any weedy tendencies. This is a clump-forming species and I find that it not only doesn't seed itself but it stays a manageable size without spreading. Its hairy leaves have chocolate-coloured spots, its bright yellow flowers float on tall stems. I grow it at the front of the Flower Garden borders nearest to the house along with other yellows – *Euphorbia polychroma* and *Euphorbia palustris* – and contrasted with the purple of alliums. By using the brilliance of colour at the front, it enhances the sense of the garden's depth. In early June, it seems the house is rising through a buttercup meadow, that the sun is lit on every cupped flower and petal. The effect lasts for some six weeks, after which I use a herbaceous sickle and cut it all to the ground for new

108

chocolate-spotted leaves to bounce back within a few weeks. By interweaving woolly buttercups through the planting, it does not leave great gaps in the border and allows the other herbaceous perennials to fill out and further the season's interest.

My early thinking about the plants I might grow was influenced by the books I read, often picked up at jumble sales or chosen at the local library, in particular those of Marjorie Fish. She was passionate about flowers and about nature, creating a garden in the English cottage style at East Lambrook Manor, beginning in 1938. I was drawn to the abundance and the relaxed informality that mixed old-fashioned and contemporary plants. The very first gardening book that I bought, though, was Christopher Lloyd's *The Well-Tempered Garden*. Looking back, it was a perfect choice, full of plant knowledge, straight talking, opinionated, expressive and well-written. It would be a long time before I actually got to visit Great Dixter but when I finally did – and I felt I already knew it through the writing – I was taken by my daughter Emma who spent a week working there for Fergus Garrett.

Then came the books of Dan Pearson, Derek Jarman and Beth Chatto, books to educate a developing gardener. When we moved house, a quarter of the sitting room was high with removals, and it was three months before we got bookcases installed. Then at long last, I was able to get my gardening books out of their cardboard boxes and it felt like greeting old friends: Christo, Dan, Monty, Derek Jarman, Gertrude…it was a pleasure to find ones that I had forgotten I had such as a little pamphlet on the Jekyll gardens of Northern England or one on working with living willow.

I delighted in setting them out on their new shelves to read whenever I want. Fourteen years on and much of my day-to-day reading is from websites, my Saturday mornings made happier by Dan Pearson's blog *DigDelve* with its calm and beautiful photographs by Huw Morgan. The theme that runs through the writings that I have enjoyed reading is of observing where a plant grows in its natural habitat and creating miniature plant communities in a garden setting. It is as Beth Chatto said a case of "right plant, right place" and of combining plants with a light touch and in the spirit of wilding, though carefully put together.

Creating the right balance between the wild and the cultivated requires a certain amount of editing. I will go through the borders in March when it is still possible to see the emerging matrix, thinning out seedlings, taking out clumps that might jostle for space and imagining how it will all look as it fills out. It is helpful to be able to visualise the effect, to know your plants intimately and what their spread and precocity will be. But it's something I do at that time of the year anyway when I am weeding the Flower Garden, laying down mulch and preparing for the months when it will be harder to get in and amongst the interweaving planting.

Then spring and summer fill it all out. The evening sunlight slides in through the sycamores, over the stone wall, to backlight the glorious undulations of flowers. The glow illuminates the campion, turning it the colour of red wine. Honesty petals flutter between skyrockets of camassia. Foxgloves become translucent and pale, and white sweet rocket dances cloud-like over peony and iris. The softness of wildflowers weaves through the borders, loose and billowy, blending and uniting, turning it all into one large meadow garden.

The Garden's Wildlife: Insects

When we came here, the land around our house was not a place for wildlife. There was no cover, nowhere to sleep or hide, no food, no worms, no insects. Just bulldozed hard ground and rubbish. Around it, the valley with its woods and fields, river, stream and marshy ground was a rich mix of habitats. From the first moments of creating a wildlife garden, there was a response. That first robin in the corkscrew hazel and that first bumblebee that lighted in a lungwort flower were the start of an unstoppable, welcome flow. The garden quickly became a hub, drawing into itself the diversity of the surrounding countryside. In a very short time, it achieved a balance so that organic gardening is possible with no one species dominating as ladybirds and hoverfly larvae eat aphids and birds forage for caterpillars. The one mammal to have boom years is the bank vole. They are very destructive, eating choice plants such as hellebore buds, nibbling unseen beneath a covering of snow or decimating the silver mats of dianthus. Frustratingly, voles will eat just the base of a stem, leaving the rest to wilt on the ground. Luckily the tawny owls know that the garden is a good place to hunt. I can watch them through the window at dusk, their rounded wings just visible against the paling sky, and be lulled to sleep as they hoot back and forth.

A wildlife garden needs to begin from the base of the food chain. The soil, which we enrich continuously with home-made compost, is now worm-rich. Thrushes tug at worms in the lawn or hop their way through the lines of vegetables. Blackbirds flick aside leaf litter with their beaks as they search for food. The banquet of choice for insects – single flowers, varieties with plenty of nectar and pollen – maximises the species that come to feed from the wide variety of garden plants.

It all starts with winter bulbs, with the snowdrops, snowflakes and aconites. It will depend on what sort of winter we have – and here in the North Pennines there can be heavy snowfalls – but if the days are warm enough, snowdrops have both nectar and yellow-orange pollen for bees at a time when there is less available. Hellebores are flourishing in our woodland border, dusky beauties that I grew from seed, growing them on in large pots before setting out forty when we first came here. They flow around the skirts of *Sarcococca confusa*, the sweet box that has small sweetly scented winter flowers and dark green leaves, a present to the garden from the editor of *The Northumbrian* magazine, where I have written a garden column for many years.

These early flowers are especially valuable to insects. Aubrieta tumbling down the retaining walls, low growing shrubs of peachy-coloured Japanese quince, ground covering lungworts and bugle, crocuses, wallflowers and an abundance of cowslips. I grow very few shrubs, preferring instead to see the rise and fall of perennials throughout the year, but there are some select varieties in the woodland border that also help to filter the westerly winds. Sumptuous dark red and tall yellow tree peonies, native junipers, sweet box, hazel and flowering redcurrant *Ribes sanguineum*. This is a favourite with bumblebees and bees, both solitary and hive bees, attracted to its dangling crimson tubular flowers. The leaves give off a pungent scent, especially on sunny days or if you rub them, and it is such a reliable shrub of old cottage gardens. I prune it just after flowering to keep it within bounds and to maximum blooms for next year's bees.

I aim to provide flowers for insects throughout most of the year. The Royal Horticultural Society conducted a four-year field study called Plants for Bugs to discover how much the geographical origin of plants affected the abundance and diversity of the invertebrates they supported. The average UK garden contains around

70 per cent of just non-native plants to 30 per cent of British native ones. The results showed that the best strategy for gardeners is to plant a mix of flowering plants from different countries and regions with an emphasis on those native to the UK. Exotic plants from the Southern Hemisphere are useful in extending the season but "the more flowers a garden can offer throughout the year, the greater number of bees, hoverflies and other pollinating insects it will attract and support".

After the early bulbs and the hellebores, it is time for the honesty, when this unpretentious biennial colours the borders in purple wherever its seeds have landed. Named for its moon-shaped, nearly see-through seedpods, *Lunaria annua* is naturalised throughout Britain, often beside paths or railway lines. It is much loved by orange-tip butterflies, *Anthocharis cardamines*, possibly my favourite butterfly because it is so uplifting and synonymous with spring. The males sport the orange on their wing tips whilst the underside of the hindwing of both males and females has delightful subtle green marbling. As well as honesty, they are attracted to two plants that I grow especially with them in mind: Jack by the hedge, *Alliaria petiolata*, also known as hedge garlic and lady's smock, or cuckooflower, *Cardamine pratensis*. The link with this food plant is there in the butterfly's specific name.

It was a wildflower, red campion, that attracted an unusual visitor in spring 2020, an example of what a hub for insects the garden has become. Although Brimstone butterflies were sights from my childhood, I had never seen one in Northumberland, where they are rarities. So it was with a bolt of recognition that I watched a large yellow butterfly in the late afternoon heat as I was putting away my gardening tools. I chased it excitedly as it jerked and kinked over the vegetables, pausing for a second on some woody cranesbill, before feeding from the red campion in my wildflower meadow.

The longest lived of our British butterflies, adult brimstones can be a year old, often overwintering amongst ivy or holly leaves. Though they mainly feed on thistles, their spring nectar sources are plants that I grow in my garden such as bugle, cowslip and campion. Their caterpillar food plants, though, are the leaves of buckthorn and alder buckthorn, neither of which are known to grow in this area and are why there are so few recorded here. There are on average just two brimstones a year in this county, hence my astonishment but pleasure too at knowing that I was growing the right flowers, at least for the adult butterflies.

As spring gathers pace, there follows a mass of plants for insects as the woodland border swells into greenery with nodding geums, spotted dead nettles, alexanders, aquilegias and honey-scented *Euphorbia amygdaloides* var. *robbiae*. The flow of flowering plants moves across the garden in a wave, west to east. Wasps feed from the dusky bells of *Nectaroscordum siculum*, bees crowd on purple alliums or hustle in blowsy peonies, hoverflies dart amongst the Mexican daisies and bumblebees nose inside blooms of pink-flowered sage. Opium poppies are a huge draw, creating frenzied activity as bees nudge each other aside during the two morning hours of their nectar flow.

It's busy in the Vegetable Garden too where the tops of the umbellifers – dill, fennel and wild carrot – become flat-topped feeding tables for beetles and hoverflies. The calendulas that David uses to encircle the vegetable beds attract beneficial insects – ladybirds, lacewings and hoverflies. The vegetables themselves are food for insects too, with broad beans being a favourite with bumblebees. French lavenders, grown close to the house wall, allow me to sit on the doorstep with a cup of tea and watch bumblebees working fast to extract their nectar, or I might hope for a hummingbird hawk-moth in the Bowles mauve wallflowers grown by the door in large, glazed pots. The sea hollies self-seeded in the gravel beds are irresistible to wasps. I grow a number of different types of sea holly but these biennials, *Eryngium giganteum* 'Silver Ghost', are a powerful attractant, as they cluster on every domed head of teasel-like flowers that sit in silver-white bracts. Bees do like them also, but it is wasps that are specially drawn to them, a reminder of what valuable pollinators they are.

Autumn is a late season feast for insects. Tall stands of purple asters are brimful with butterflies, reminding me of how I would gaze up at them as a child, mesmerised by peacocks, red admirals and commas. Of the white-edged square Instamatic photos where I attempted to capture the feeling of watching them and had to wait weeks to have returned to me in folded flap packets. Then there's bugbane, every white firework of a flower spike crowded with flies and butterflies lured by its scent, an almost nauseous sweetness.

The final smorgasbord of sedums makes for an incredible journey for anyone walking down the central path. Butterflies fly restlessly up to settle again further along the line. There are rich warm tones from the wings of small coppers, red admirals and commas, peacocks and small tortoiseshells. Bumblebees barely move, greedy for the plentiful nectar before winter. Many different species of fly also visit the small candy-pink stars that *en masse* make up the large flowerheads.

The sedums are also visited by the day-flying silver Y moth, *Plusia gamma*. People sometimes mistake these for hummingbird hawk-moths since they are also a blur of rapid wings and it is the UK's most common migrant moth. We see them here in late summer and autumn, often on the long line of catmint down the central path. If their wings ever hold still for long enough, you can see the silver hook-shaped marking on the marbled grey-brown forewing that gives it its name. Recent research shows that they migrate at altitudes of up to 1.2km.

Every week between March and November, I set a light-trap to find out which moths are present in the garden. As each year goes by, the information increases in value as patterns and trends emerge, the data being submitted to the National Moth Recording Scheme and the Garden Moth Scheme. One year, I took part in the winter as well. Although more moths were recorded here than at any other location in Northumberland, I found that I preferred to have a winter break and not have to put out the trap in the snow. There are a number of different systems for moth trapping but I use a Robinson 125w with a mercury vapour bulb. Moths are attracted by its powerful light and funnelled down into a large black tub below from which it is harder for them to find their way out. Inside are egg boxes giving plenty of places for insects to hide. There are often beetles, wasps, stone flies and others in there as well, adding to the fascination. I set the trap just before dusk and turn the light off as soon after dawn as I can manage, hoping to do so before a robin or wren wakes up to an easy meal.

Moth trapping is addictive. That early morning moment of discovery is like opening a treasure chest full of expectation and surprise. First, I check the walls and paving for any moths that have settled outside the trap. Some are so well camouflaged against moss and lichen that I have to scan the area with care, taking any photographs as a record in case they fly off. Then comes the moment of reveal, the hope for a species that I haven't yet recorded, the thrill of meeting old friends for the first time that year. It has become part of my telling of the seasons, the first Hebrew characters of spring, the exotic hawk-moths of summer, the November moths of autumn.

Butterflies and moths are closely related, but butterflies have clubbed antennae whereas moths, with the exception of burnet moths, do not. Their caterpillars are an important food source for birds, those of the winter moth being collected from the tree

canopy by great tits and blue tits for feeding their chicks. The
birds' breeding season is timed to coincide with this emergence,
an example of the interconnectedness and impact on birds of
changing climate. These are the pale green caterpillars that you
can see dangling on a silken thread from branches. A single brood
of blue tits can be fed up to 10,000 winter moth caterpillars.

Winter moth adults have pale grey wings and could easily
be overlooked in their drabness. They might accord with many
people's ideas of moths – dull and uninteresting like the brown
house moth that eats holes in jumpers. But show someone the
morning contents of a moth trap and they are astounded at what
beautifully patterned and varied insects have been flying unno-
ticed in the night. Canary-shouldered thorn like a glamorous
diva with a yellow feather boa thrown round her neck. Mother
of pearl with its soft nacreous marbling. Dramatic scarlet tigers,
white spots on jet black and flashes of red underwings. Burnished
brass shining metallically from different angles. Poplar hawk-
moths with sculpted blush-grey wings, sending out signals from
red patches on their underwings if they feel threatened. With
their size and colour, these are good species to show the wonder
of moths to children.

Their names are evocative too. These are often descriptive of
their markings such as pebble hook-tip, dark arches, gold spangle
or antler. But there are also wonderful flights of fancy – Merveille
du Jour, old lady, lobster moth and gypsy moth. Because many
were named by Victorian naturalists, they often recall life in the
big house with its wainscots, footmen, brocades, heralds, satins
and ermines. Maybe a puzzle on naming led to the moth known
as the confused. Look at the delightful spectacle face-on and the
white hairs that ring its eyes do indeed look like a pair of specs.
Even though I encounter this moth many times in the season, I
find it impossible not to smile when I turn it around to look at it

from the front.

Some moths use mimicry for protection such as the beautiful buff-tip that imitates a broken-off birch twig or red sword-grass a sliver of wood. The curious looking Chinese character with its silver, brown and grey mottling is camouflaged to look like a bird dropping. Mottled beauty is easy to miss against a background of leaf litter or wood. The peppered moth with its salt and pepper markings is an example of evolution in action. Both a light and a dark form are attracted to my moth trap, most often resting on the wall next to it where their wings are a perfect imitation of lichen or tree bark. A dark – melanic – form was discovered in Manchester in 1848 and this became the dominant form of the local population since it was less easily seen against the soot-blackened backgrounds of the Industrial Revolution. As air pollution lessened over the twentieth century, the light form was less likely to be picked out by birds in the cleaner environment.

After I have checked the moth trap and noted the different species, I cover it and leave it in a cool shed for the day so that they can be released at night unharmed. Other frequent visitors to the trap are colourful sexton beetles, *Nicrophorus vespilloides*, their chunky bodies banded in orange and black and often carrying a number of small orange mites that hitch a ride to the carrion. There's a number of these burying beetles in the UK that bury dead animals such as mice and birds by excavating the soil beneath the body so that it sinks into the earth. They then lay their eggs and the rotting animal becomes a food supply for their larvae. It is fascinating to watch this happening as I did with a pair of sexton beetles burying a dead hedgehog over a few weeks until there was no surface trace. One time, I watched sexton beetles attempting to dig beneath a dead vole except that this was impossible because it was lying on a paving slab. I moved both vole and beetles into a border where they could carry on their work of recycling.

As the summer lengthens, there are dragonflies in the Vegetable Garden close by the river. A common hawker buzzes me, settling on my striped T-shirt. There's plenty of water in the valley with the River Allen and the streams that feed into it, but I wanted to have some still water within the garden, a place to watch birds drink or peer into for diving beetles and other pond life. Buying an old farm drinking trough from a friend, we set this on a gravelled area in the back terrace, ideal for breaking up what had been too large an area of paving. Painting it black inside, I planted up a mesh basket at one end with bogbean, *Menyanthes trifoliata*, a native wildflower found mostly in Scotland. Its common name comes from its three-part leaves that look like those of broad beans, and it grows in lochs marshes and bogs and has feathery white star flowers with pink-tinged petals. Another name is boghop from its past use in flavouring beer.

The trough pond is a delight, its smooth surface reflecting the sky. Its long thin shape works perfectly in the rectangular space of the terrace. On its south side, I have planted a simple line of just one iris. Iris 'Banbury Ruffles' grows no taller than the trough, its glaucous leaves and frilly deep violet-blue flowers just right in front of the galvanised grey. All around, allowed to self-seed between the stone paviours, are lamb's ears, their silver spires with tiny pink flowers, a summer-long feast for insects. Buddleias edge the terrace, their scent drawing bees and butterflies. Pots of cosmos, agapanthus and nicotiana stand either side of a large bench. It's a paradise for pollinators.

All season long, this huge restless mass of insects makes the garden pulsate with life. If I visit a garden that relies on superbred plants that are of little or no benefit to pollinators, I am struck by the dramatic contrast. Created to be showy, the modifications in their breeding make them inaccessible to insects. I look at the huge long-lasting colourful blooms of begonias and double French marigolds and I see something akin to plastic flowers. They feel dead, bought for their colour but probably without realising that they do nothing at all for insects – and therefore for birds, mammals and all the other wildlife that makes a garden feel alive.

The Garden's Wildlife: Birds

Insects form the essential base of the garden habitat pyramid. They provide food for all those other creatures that people like to watch around their homes, and especially for birds. From my kitchen window, I might see a spotted flycatcher sweep out from a branch in an aerial pass to quickly snatch an insect and land back in the tree. Or watch a blackbird feed its fledgling with bunches of worms on the coping stone of a wall. Pied wagtails, *Motacilla alba*, bob-bob along the stone roof of the house and grey wagtails fly up the burn. Wrens pick tiny spiders from around the wooden edge of the window, unaware that I am standing just inside. Redstarts sing from the top of the ash tree just outside the garden and one year nested in a cavity in the shed wall. Jays chatter and squabble, flying with a flash of kingfisher-blue wings. A great spotted woodpecker works its way up the trunk of the sycamore, tap-tapping in a search for grubs in crevices in the bark. Sitting in the garden, I am lulled by soft crooning calls of pigeons and the stock doves that nest in the prickly depths of the hawthorn.

It's the hawthorns in winter that have berries for birds as hungry blackbirds and thrushes pick the wrinkled red fruits from their spiny branches. A cold winter will see redwings come down into the valley bottom, migrants from Scandinavia with cream stripes above their eyes and orange-red flanks. I watch from the kitchen window as they lean forward on thin branches that barely hold their weight, desperate to pluck the haws from the ends of twigs. On a winter walk, I startle woodcock, *Scolopax rusticola*, from the base of gorse bushes, only flying up at the very last moment. In spring, I can step outside the back door at dusk to watch the male woodcocks roding in a breeding display flight as they patrol around the wood. Though they are only just visible against a darkening sky, I can see their beautiful long bills and rapid wing beats, and hear their strange mixture of low grunts and squeaking calls. But for exquisite song, nothing can match the song thrush belting out its loud repeated clear phrases from the top of the ash tree by the house, or the excitement of hearing the first cuckoo. I can be fully absorbed in weeding a border and unprepared for this significant spring moment. That magical double note will instantly feed into my thoughts and I'll straighten up to listen, elated that it's another year with a cuckoo in the valley.

Thanks to decades of bird ringing and, more recently, satellite tracking, we know that cuckoos go to Africa for the winter, crossing the Sahara in one long continuous flight. The migration route is fraught with difficulties from drought, lack of food or being killed. Then there's habitat loss as well as fewer insects for food and it is not surprising that the cuckoo is in severe decline. This makes me all the more relieved when I hear the first of the season, or even better, because they are often hard to spot, I watch a cuckoo fly across the field from one wood to another. They come because their host species can be found here; they lay their eggs in the nests of the valley's reed warblers, dunnocks or meadow pipits on the moorland higher up. Only males utter the distinctive call, opening their bills for the "cuck" and closing them for the resonant "oo". If you can imitate this well enough, you can draw a competitive male to you; I tried this once and had a furious male cuckoo fly straight into a tree near where I was standing, looking for his rival.

Picking sweet peas in the Vegetable Garden early one morning, I was alerted by blackbird alarm calls and noticed what seemed a bird of prey on the stone wall by the river. Rushing for binoculars, I could watch it from the house – a young cuckoo. It stayed around all day, coming as close to the house as the terrace or flying silently across the vegetable rows, straight as a raptor, being mobbed by small birds. Jays screeched and a jackdaw stood sentry on the chimney pot. After supper, we sat in the summer-house when, glancing out of the window, I saw it perched on the crossbar of the runner bean poles, clutching with yellow talons, barred chest facing me as I very slowly raised my camera to grab the moment.

Insects provide food for dunnocks, meadow pipits and warblers, and therefore support cuckoos. Smaller birds provide food for birds of prey. A flurry of panicked wings and the frantic calls of agitated blackbirds means a sparrowhawk has swept into the garden. Kestrels hover over the rough grass of the field or use the solitary hawthorn as a viewpoint. A peregrine once stopped briefly, using the finial of the summerhouse as a perch, and an unusual visitor to a neighbouring garden was a young merlin come down from the higher ground. Red kites occasionally pass along the valley, but it is the buzzards that we see all year round.

Common buzzards, *Buteo buteo*, fly high above all these birds, above valley, field, river and two figures working their garden. They rise and circle on thermals of air, launching off from the top of the wooded bank, broad wings showing pale against the sky, rich brown cloaking their shoulders. Buzzards barely flap their wings whilst gliding. Their wing tips are dark and splayed, yellow legs tucked beneath their bodies, head turning this way and that as they hunt for food. Mostly, this is for earthworms and carrion such as a dead rabbit on the track, perhaps beetles or frogs, making it quite common to see a buzzard stood on a fence post or down on the ground. As they launch themselves into the air from the top of a tree, they utter a drawn-out, plaintiff mewing. It's this that makes me look up, shading my eyes, to be completely absorbed for a moment in the slow movement above my head. I've seen as many as seven buzzards at once and can watch them throughout the seasons.

Buzzards are often unable to go about their business without being mobbed by other species that see them as a threat. The mewing that makes me look up can be when a buzzard is being dive-bombed by crows or other birds; it always sounds to me like a protest to be left alone. It may be that a pair of curlews are defending their nest amongst the tussocks of grass in the field below, their urgent alarm calls mixing with the lazier sound of the raptor. The buzzards' courtship display is thrilling and often takes place over our house. A male climbs up swiftly, folds his wings back and stoops in a daredevil rollercoaster flight. The pair tumble together, locking their claws, and spiralling down. In *The Love Games of Buzzards*, poet Robin Moss writes, "tangling their talons, knotting tenderly, then like twine unspooling, falling towards the valley's green sheets". There's something very beautiful about using those powerful and destructive claws with delicacy for bonding. All year round, the call of buzzards echoes round the valley and they are part of the wildlife that makes this place so special.

Night times are never quiet. There is the ever-present sound of the river, sometimes loud but mostly a background hum. Bats rustle beneath the roof, a pheasant clacks loudly from the field. The owls call across the darkened garden, mostly at dusk and dawn but also in spells during the night. I find their drawn-out hooting carries me along if I can't sleep and I think of the words of Dylan Thomas in *Fern Hill*, "As I rode to sleep the owls were bearing the farm away."

A couple of years after we moved here, my son made a tawny owl box for me as a birthday present. There are two basic templates for this, upright and sloping, both mimicking hollow branches. He made his to the sloping design and set it at a 45-degree angle in the sycamore above the woodland border. It took a while for it to be occupied but there has now been a brood for a few years. I first realised that something was happening because of a daytime clamour of agitated tits and dunnocks. A female tawny owl stood on a projecting branch, the bark scuffed by her talons. I had heard her calling with loud "kee-wicks" in the deep of night, but this was confirmation that she was using our box. She blended with the foliage, leaf patterns dancing shadows over her mottled plumage, sometimes sleeping, sometimes looking straight at me with unreadable black eyes. She learnt our movements and I could garden nearby or notice her become alert at the sound of a door opening before she'd relax again. If anyone else was about, she would retreat deep into branches. My weeding or hoeing didn't seem to bother her. I would look sideways at her, so it wasn't obvious that I was watching, even being able to see her beak open like a yawn and see the pink inside of her mouth.

Some years, there was one chick in the box, sometimes two. The female would spend her days outside but, as the light dimmed, I could just make out her first hunting flight of the night. In late June, it must get hot and stuffy in the wooden box and the chicks don't wait until night to start exploring. There, peeping over the lip of the box, are two pale grey chicks, staring at me with ebony eyes. Before they can fly, chicks explore their new environment by branching, scrabbling up and down tree trunks as they learn, jumping, fluttering and using their sharp claws. If they fall to the ground, they can walk back up the trunk. They beg noisily for food and the adults will feed them on the ground. Our owlets would be active in the daytime and I could watch as they comically hopped along the coping stones of the wall.

One night, we came home as it was getting dark and an owlet was standing on the willow fence just outside the kitchen window. We passed quickly by but I sat in the darkened room, looking out of the window as, after a quarter of an hour, it started to relax from its frozen state. A twisting of its head, a scratch amongst feathers, a loud peep demanding food. In the dim light, an owl flew in, landing next to the youngster, and I watched as it passed over a vole into the owlet's open beak; even amongst the daily wildlife of this place, it was an extraordinary moment.

I can have close meetings with some of these visitors. A robin will follow me round the garden. As I stand still, straightening from turning over the soil, it will hop between my feet, pecking insects from the top of my boots and darting around my legs. When wrens fledge, they often explode out of the nest in all directions, a defensive strategy to confound predators. Passing by a tangle of hawthorn branches at just the right moment, I saw a flurry of newly emerged wrens exploring the world outside the nest. A parent was calling frenziedly from a nearby tree when one of the fledglings flew up and stood on my shoulder. I slowly turned my head to look at it, but I could feel nothing through my shirt, weighing as they do no more than a pound coin.

With the varied habitats around the house, that mixture of field woods and river, the bird life is equally varied. This can lead to close encounters with species that are normally quite shy. Hearing a strange guttural sound, half quacking, halfgrunting, I walked quietly to the burnside wall to look down at the stream. A goosander chick was trying to clamber up the steep step of the waterfall but the mother was trying to entice it in the other direction. There, swimming downstream, was a female goosander followed by a flotilla of ten chicks that she was anxiously hurrying down to the main river. Goosanders, sleek handsome birds, speedy in the water and equipped with sawbills for catching slippery fish, nest in holes in trees, so I imagine that the family had just fledged and left the wood higher up the burn. It is these everyday yet exceptional moments that make living here amongst wildlife so very special.

Though we are tucked down in the valley, we still hear the cries of moorland birds. Peewits fly overhead; they nest in the fields above us. Curlews feed in the meadow across the river. But to fully experience the sounds of wading birds, we will go for a walk on the moors and rough fields above Allendale. Here, hidden amongst the field rushes, they lay their eggs. The rushes that grow in damp places provide tussocky growth to hide nest and chicks but they need to be in the right balance to grass – less than two-thirds of the field area – to meet the needs both of wildlife and grazing land. A spring walk is filled with their evocative cries, along with strident oystercatchers, flocks of golden plover, pee-wits, redshank and snipe.

It's very hard to spot snipe, camouflaged as they are amongst the rushes, their brown streaked backs resembling dead grass stems. Like woodcock, they lie low until you are almost on top of them before suddenly lifting. When snipe conduct their display flight, they are hard to see against the sky, in the same way that it's hard to spot a singing lark. Once you pinpoint one, though, it's exhilarating to watch a snipe drumming, plummeting and swoop-ing with its tail feathers vibrating in the wind, creating a whirring mechanical sound.

Our favourite springtime walk is up a sandy track between rushy fields and out onto the open moor. We go because of the birdsong. The air is filled with the sound of larks, singing like ventriloquists from different places than you expect them to be. An intense, sweet warbling in continuous streams of sound. Displaying peewits cry "wee weep weep weep" as they soar and tumble over clumps of field rush. There's the sad, peeping single notes of golden plover like a kitten begging for food, the high piping calls of meadow pipit, the piercing alarm call of redshank and snipe drumming high above us. And best of all, a gliding curlew bursts out in jubilant bubbling, my spirits rising with it. It's the spring soundscape of waders returned to the Allen Valleys to breed and we return home uplifted, full and happy.

These moors are managed for the red grouse that eat the young shoots of heather. As we walk, they fly up, often from almost under our feet, with their strange calls of "Go back! Go back! Go back!" Rarer, but also here in Allendale, are black grouse, *Tetrao tetrix*, larger birds that are always thrilling to see. When I first came to Northumberland, I lived in a remote cottage in Wark Forest where water had to be collected from a spring across a field. It was a half-hour walk to where I was working on a dig on Hadrian's Wall (fresh from art college, I was drawing the site plans) but a slow potholed seventeen miles round by road. This took me past a black grouse lek where I'd see the males posturing and strutting in an open area in the forest, unaware at the time just how special this sight was. They generally begin lekking at dawn but I would see them on my way to work.

Male black grouse have jet-black feathers, a red wattle over their eyes and a flash of white from beneath their lyre-shaped tails. The muted colouring of the females is better for camouflage and they are known as grey hens. Lek sites are traditional and go back many years, which is why it is so important that they are not disturbed. They gather at these sites throughout the year with the peak of activity in April and May when females wait to select their mates, rather like the deer rut. Males compete for the most prominent central position on the site with bubbling calls, flutter-jumping and fanning out their tails to exhibit their startlingly white under-tail feathers. It's a spectacular display, all the more exciting for being rare.

Black grouse feed on the ground for much of the year, eating shoots of heather and bilberry, grasses and wildflowers, feeding insects and spiders to their chicks. But when winter weather hits, they are up in the trees after berries. With their large size, there is something comical and unexpected about seeing black grouse amongst the branches of the hawthorns that line the roads in and out of the valley.

Between the waders breeding on the moors, cuckoos calling in our valley, black grouse in winter and our plentiful garden birds, the year here revolves around rhythms and cycles, familiar patterns giving reassurance in unsettling times. The looked-for annual events, the seasonal comings and goings, mark changes in the year. The first swallow is an ecstatic moment and a feeling of homecoming, their autumn departure an empty sky day. From July, the curlews leave, heading west, perhaps to the Solway, a flock so high up that I can't see them but can hear them speaking to each other as they fly. It fills me with sweet sadness and a sense of loss. Their voices won't be heard in Allendale for many months and I will have to go to the coast to hear curlews calling, until next spring.

The Garden's Wildlife: Mammals

The wildlife seen from the house can be distracting when I'm writing at my desk. A troupe of long-tailed tits might do acrobatics through the ash tree out of the window or a discreet little treecreeper tap and claw its way up the trunk. It can be distracting also when I'm on the phone. It's winter and I answer it, moving to the front window where I see a stoat running fluidly across the bare ground. Svelte and sinuous, white-chested with a rufous black-tipped tail. The stoat zigzags across the front garden, nipping in and out of any perennials that are left standing for their seedheads, quartering the ground like a barn owl across a field, hunting with strategy.

I move to another window to watch it flowing down the low retaining wall, running nimbly along the bars of the cattle grid, searching in the dark recesses. Across the gravel garden, up the side of the old chimney pot to peer into it, then up the side of a stone wall, along its top, down onto the lawn, onto the back terrace to cling to the underside of the Lutyens bench, by which time I'm at the back landing window. Up another stone wall, into the meadow, up the willow tree, investigating each branch before it disappears back down into the garden. In the process of one phone call, I've gone to every upstairs window, following the path of this vital and lithe animal.

Some years, the stoats turn white and I see an ermine in the garden. It's usually only those that live on higher ground that change the colour of their coats in winter for camouflage in a snowy landscape. The transformation is triggered by shorter day length and the process – as well as changing back to the normal red-brown – takes some weeks. During that time, a stoat will have a patchy coat, and in years when there is no snow, the effect is counterproductive and an ermine stands out very visibly in the landscape. In fourteen years, we have been thoroughly snowed in three times but have had some snow most winters. Ermine fur is luxuriously dense and this made it the animal pelt chosen for the robes of royalty and the church.

Stoats rear their kits within the dry-stone walls or sometimes in our log pile where, come autumn, I might find a downy nest lined with rabbit fur. Of the one litter a year, they can have between six and twelve kits. They are reared on a diet of rabbits, voles, mice and rats as well as birds and their eggs. They are lithe enough to slip down a burrow or into a nest in a hole in a tree. A stoat can drag a rabbit that is several times heavier than it, even over a stone wall, though I once saw a defiant rabbit chase away a stoat that was trying to get into its burrow. Watching the young stoats play is a joy. They race and tumble over each other, flicking their black-tipped tails, standing bolt upright on their back legs, learning to hunt through the energy of play.

Our human boundaries are illusory. Though they keep out farm animals, wildlife flows in and through them. They are semi-permeable boundaries through which stoat, vole and wren can pass. They provide nest sites, safety, food and shelter, and are made from stones that come from the land around. Lichens, mosses and ferns grow on their grey limestone surfaces and cobwebs stretch between them, jewelled by water droplets on early mornings. That's when I take out my close-up binoculars that can focus in to just 50cm and lose myself in the miniature landscape of foliose lichens and tiny forests of moss.

Voles scurry between the gaps in the dry-stone walls or make their burrows behind the stones of the low retaining wall of the Flower Garden. If there is a thick covering of snow, they create snaking corridors beneath its surface, scuttling along out of danger from hunting owls. If the snow lies for days, this lack of food can have a serious effect on the owl population. It also means that the voles will eat my plants under the snow, chewing hellebores and winter irises, killing clematis and doing lots of damage. Three to four litters a year and as many as five young in each litter add up to a lot of voles. There are gaps beneath the paving slabs and the voles exploit this too. On a day of heavy rain, we watched from the window as a vole carried its young to safety one at a time, each dangling from its mouth, away from the rising water and into a dry wall. There are shrews and field mice in the garden too, taking advantage of the relative safety of the meadow edges to the lawn.

It's in this quiet area of long grass that I choose to release hedgehogs. Over the years, we have received twenty-one of these delightful but sadly endangered creatures, arriving in cardboard boxes from Northumbrian Hedgehog Rescue Trust. Scarred by accidents or found underweight before winter, they have been rehabilitated at the centre, a place that manages solely on donations. Our garden is a perfect release site because there are no cars, no dogs and no badgers. It often surprises people but badgers are the main natural predators of hedgehogs in the UK, eating them from underneath and discarding the spiny skin.

Hedgehogs have everything they need in this garden from secluded shelter to natural food and water, but they are also capable of climbing and will have ebbed out into the valley where there are reports of neighbours feeding hedgehogs in their gardens. The hedgehogs would arrive in the back of a hatchback, brought by a volunteer. Each box was labelled with the hedgehogs' names and had breathing holes, taped up doors, bedding of shredded paper, dried food and water. We took them to quiet parts of the garden and left them there until dusk. I left out some cat food, meat- not fish-based, and bowls of water before opening the doors of the boxes at dusk. A half moon cast shadows across the garden, bats flew around the roof of the house and tawny owls began calling to each other in the wood. I sat motionless and watched as the most adventurous of the hedgehogs emerged. It slowly investigated its new surroundings, nosing through the undergrowth, snuffling at smells on the path, tucking into the food bowl. By morning, all the boxes were empty, the shredded paper seemed to have exploded out of the doors and all the food had been eaten. They disappeared into the thick cover of the borders but it was reassuring to notice black droppings on the paths and lawns, a sign that they were still about.

Every autumn, I collect up all the leaves from paths and terraces and lay them thickly over the woodland border. Here, amongst arching hellebore leaves and evergreen epimediums, a hedgehog can overwinter, creating a hibernaculum that looks like an upturned bucket of leaves. These insulated mounds keep a steady temperature inside. Look carefully at this heap of leaves and small twigs and you can see that there is method in its construction where the hedgehog has carried them in its mouth and placed them one on top of another. The other area that they will use to shelter is beneath the dry covering mound of grasses, *Stipa gigantea* and pampas, a warning to take care when raking out the old thatch in spring.

Of the larger mammals, it would be hard to make a garden with badgers as they root in lawns and borders, digging with their sharp claws. Luckily, perhaps, I've only once seen a badger in the valley but had some close encounters in other places in Northumberland. In that first summer that I moved to the north to work on the Roman dig on Hadrian's Wall, I was taken badger watching by a ranger with the Northumberland National Park. Climbing into the spreading branches of an oak tree in Hareshaw Dene, we waited one evening near to a sett. I was in my early twenties and it was the first time that I'd seen badgers behaving naturally: ambling, scuffling, scratching their tummies, unaware of the watchers.

Later, when I lived in a farm cottage, I regularly sat in an alder above a stream-side sett to the point where the badgers were familiar with my scent. Cubs would rough and tumble in play or adults clean the old bedding out of the sloping earth entrance and drag new hay into the hole of the sett. The alder was not very high off the ground and I had long hair down to my waist. One time, the person sitting in the tree a little above me looked down to see a male badger that came up and nosed my hair. Unperturbed, it carried on its evening.

Badgers can be very feisty, and one evening we were walking back across the field and met a youngster, only realising what it was in the dim light before we could avoid it. Half rolling onto its back, it snarled ferociously, baring its teeth, as we quickly backed off. That same night, as we were going quietly along a sunk lane, two fox cubs were playing on the ground just above us, seen through the light screen of a hedge and oblivious in their fervour.

Deer would also make gardening very difficult. In the fourteen years that we have been here, the population of roe deer in the valley has tripled and they have become more used to people. When we first moved to this house, I had to slip carefully through the woods to look down on three deer lying up in a hidden dell. They are now almost daily sights out in the open, running down to the river to drink, browsing the hillside or bounding in front of my car. From a standing start, a deer can leap the barbed wire fence that keeps the sheep from the woodland. A flash of white rump and it's disappeared into the dark of the trees.

Given a choice, deer don't like feeding in the same field as sheep or cattle. They might pass through but they tend not to stay, so we see them more in winter when there's no stock in the fields. It's with mixed feelings as a gardener and naturalist that I watch a roe buck close to our house, ears twitching back and forth, head upright scenting, but bold as brass. Over those fourteen years, there had been no deer in the garden, so it was a shock one morning to look out of the window and see a large animal wandering along the path. Powdery snow had been swept from the fields by high winds, leaving a four-foot snow drift in the lowest part of the wall by the Flower Garden. Hoof prints showed where it had been easy to walk up this and to explore the garden. Alarmed when I rushed out of the house, it sped off.

To link garden and landscape, we had decided against a perimeter hedge, so outside the wall – easily vaulted by a deer – is a barbed wire fence. There is a metre gap between the two, enough to stop cattle pushing against the stone wall and a deterrent to deer who do not want to make the wider leap. I can only hope that the deer that wandered in on the snow drift does not hold it in its memory, and luckily there was little to eat in February. Deer particularly like to browse on roses, tulips and yew. Friends who garden in Cumbria have to net their yew hedges every winter because of experiences of deer eating them right back to bare branches. There are moles, aphids, voles, mice, caterpillars, moulds and damaging weather to tackle, but it is hard to make a garden with deer!

The Greenhouse

We have a short growing season so it was obvious from the beginning that we would need a greenhouse; a place to sow seeds, to raise young plants and to get a head start. The mangled remains of a polytunnel, all twisted metal and torn polythene, amongst the rubbish and weeds when we first came here convinced us, even if we had considered it a choice, that we did not want a plastic structure. It would go against our ethos of keeping to the simple organic materials of the valley and create waste at the end of its usefulness. Only a wooden greenhouse would look right in this setting, its rectangular proportions a glass echo of the house itself.

Greenhouses come in a great variety of shapes and sizes, and one place to get inspiration and ideas is to visit an allotment. I've always loved allotments. There is such variety of self-expression and creativity in their patchwork of small gardens. I love the eclectic mix of sheds, compost bins and old baths used as water butts, of snaking paths and straight paths, of quirkiness and wildness. Looking down onto their patchwork of plots has always been one of my favourite sights on a train journey. Walking round them, you have many chance meetings. There are knowledgeable gardeners and others just starting out. Allotments bring together people of all ages and cultures, and throughout the pandemic have provided a place of refuge and solace.

The greenhouses you see there are a fascinating mixture of the homemade and the bought. It's the recycled, inventive ones that I find most interesting. A friend of mine has volunteered for many years on a school allotment in Newcastle. In 2022, Jenny Wigston won the Community Award from the RHS for the length of time she has run the West Jesmond Primary School allotment. There, amongst the lines of veg in raised beds, the wildlife pond and the wheelbarrows, is a greenhouse for the summer growing of tomatoes and chillies that reuses Perspex panels from an old telephone box. You can still see the logo of the high-stepping piper, hand raised, the red and blue fading in the city light. On some allotments, there are homemade buildings that are half shed, half greenhouse, a mixture of painted wood and glass or Perspex, old windows of various sizes, even salvaged fanlights. We, though, were in a hurry to get up and running with the new garden as well as needing a structure that fitted with the roofline and shape of the old stone house. We needed an archetypal greenhouse that would be functional and beautiful.

The best place to site a greenhouse is in an open sunny position and orientated east to west. We could manage openness and bright light but it made visual sense to set it at a 90-degree angle to the main Flower Garden path. Angling the ridge north-south, though, would help somewhat in giving an equal amount of sun in the summer months. It would just make it take longer to warm up in winter. The chosen greenhouse in western red cedar, a durable wood, had good internal space, three doors for extra ventilation and a small porch. Painted white with a couple of decorative finials, it looked traditional enough to go with the old house and was made in Darlington by Amdega. David undertook to make the base, a complicated job because it would only be a support for the walls, freeing up the internal space for planting a yearly tomato crop. If the measurements and levelling were not exact, the walls would be out of sync, so he had to make accurate wooden shuttering for the concrete.

It was March when the greenhouse was delivered, a time when the oystercatchers were back on the river, looking for gravelly places to nest. The structure had to be transferred from the huge Amdega wagon onto a flatbed trailer that would be able to come down the track. I had to go to a meeting about the hay meadows booklet on which I was collaborating with artist Kim Lewis and I was away all day. I came home at teatime to find the wooden base and doors already up. The next day, the roof went on and it took shape, white painted wood panelling, glazing bars and roof spars, bright in the developing March garden. The men who put it up so professionally, Tony and Bill, had worked for Amdega for forty and thirty-two years respectively, so I was saddened when, not long after, the company folded. The new greenhouse looked perfect in its setting, a focal point at the end of the long path.

It was frustratingly windy for several days afterwards and although I wanted to get the staging into the greenhouse and to start seed sowing, it had to wait. Doors would bang in the gales and even our wheelbarrows were being blown over. But looking out of the window through squalls of snow, I was delighted to see a pair of partridges tripping a dance on the back terrace. When the winds eased, David was able to put down rubble, then hogging and gravel in the new greenhouse where the staging was to go. Down the centre, a path of the same limestone paving slabs as our terraces. Then the wooden staging could go in, four independent units beautifully made from western red cedar with slats beneath on which to put stacks of pots. It was beginning to look like a working greenhouse. Two pots of agaves, much the worse for wear, could finally be given shelter. These had been left outside all winter, close by the wall of the house and well fleeced, but the temperature had been as low as -18. I cut off any blackened or sodden leaves, but they were still alive and each had an offset tucked away under the old growth.

The key to the survival of the agaves was probably that they were kept very dry in the rain shadow of the wall. I still have these original plants, added to by variegated agaves, and they overwinter in the greenhouse each year before standing out on

139

the terrace for the summer. I nip off the tip of their viciously spined leaves in case of eye injury when bending down near them. Their glaucous colouring and rhythmic shapes contrast with the fluidity of the Mexican daisies that froth around the feet of the pots.

The greenhouse is vital not just for seed sowing and bringing on young plants but protecting tender plants such as agave through the winter. It is unheated, being too far from the house, and we have found that the best way of keeping the plants alive is to plunge them in the soil and cover them with fleece according to the forecast. The temperature in the greenhouse in the very coldest times is usually two or three degrees higher than outside so it still gets frost inside. I take small specimens of the most tender plants onto a house windowsill as starters for propagation in case of losses. It's the only way of keeping a core of echeverias, aeoniums, argyranthemums and heliotropes, winters being so unpredictable.

Succulents, such as the echeverias, have plump, fleshy leaves in which they can store water in arid conditions. They are a world away from the rest of the planting in our garden, from the softly flowing wildflowers and perennials, yet they don't seem to jar with the overall scheme. I barely water them in winter, but left outside for the summer in pots on the terrace, they don't mind the rain, perhaps because they are in a mixture of half gravel, half compost and topped with a gravel mulch. They have rhythmic structure with leaves spiralling out from a tight centre. Cool to the touch, some are pale jade green with tiny pink tips to the end of pointed leaves, others are a deeper glaucous colour.

I was about ten years old when I bought a small plant of kalanchoe at a sale. Fascinated by the baby platelets that grew along its edges, I broke them off and started growing them on. Known as mother of thousands for good reason, they easily rooted and multiplied fast until all the windowsills were packed with them; my mother wasn't very pleased. It was another of those magic moments that showed me the thrill of propagating my own plants. Another plant that I picked up a jumble sale was the spider plant, *Chlorophytum comosum*. This produces offshoots on the ends of wiry stems, and again they are easily rooted to the point where I added to the kalanchoe-filled windowsills with the cascading variegated leaves of spider plants. Children often become interested in gardening through houseplants or cacti, perhaps because they are manageable in their indoor pots, a gateway into a love for life. I don't grow houseplants now – there is plenty to look at and to do outside – but our windowsills become the refuge for these tender plants in winter.

The greenhouse soil is where the tomato crop is grown, the cucumbers are raised and a few permanent plants sit around the edge: orange-scented thyme, French tarragon and the pale yellow snapdragons of *Asarina procumbens* that sprawl across the paving. David replenishes the top layer of soil each year, swapping it for that in the Vegetable Garden, enriching it with home-made compost and feeding the tomatoes with liquid seaweed. There's a wicker chair to sit in and a child's fishing net on a long bamboo cane to rescue bees that can't find their way out. He made a potting bench from old tree stakes and plywood packaging, and plant labels and pens are held in mugs that have lost their handles. The warm wood of the potting bench is perfect for our snoozing cat.

Nighttime temperatures can dip in the valley by as much as two degrees lower than the farm at the top. This often happens at the end of the night; we can wake to it being -3 and in that first hour of light see it drop to -5 as the cold air pools down the hillside and into the bottom. This makes a greenhouse especially important for raising young plants that can then be set outside once it warms up. We need to have a head start with vegetables in particular because the weather can cut in at the other end of the season too. Frosts are possible in September, though in some blissful years there haven't been any until late October.

There's no point in starting too soon, though. We find that sowing from February onwards – in colder years, from March – bears the same results as earlier sowings as increased warmth helps the plants catch up. First are hardy annuals such as sweet peas and calendulas and lastly tender cosmos and nicotiana. We use plug trays, reusing plastic ones that are now ten to fifteen years old but hoping that plastic alternatives come on the market sometime. For large seeds such as runner beans, we make paper pots using a wooden form. These degrade and the young bean plants can be lined out without root disturbance. The plugs are mostly grown on in 7cm-square pots, or for fast growers such as nicotiana in one-litre pots.

Washing the greenhouse glass is a long job and never feels very rewarding at the time but, as well as benefiting the plants, the increased light makes it a good place to sit. Snug in here on cool days, I can look out on to the haugh where the pheasants strut and posture, the deer bound down to the river and the kestrel stakes out the field from the topmost branch of the hawthorn. I can watch the comings and goings of the birds that nest in the voluminous old viburnum: dunnock, blackbird and blue tit. On hot days, when the doors are open, a wren will slip quietly in, fossicking amongst the stacks of plant trays on the search for tiny insects and spiders. I sit still not to panic it whilst it moves, mouse-like, amongst foliage or along the window ledges. Bees and butterflies find their way in but can't find the exit. I let them feed amongst the cherry pie plants, the thyme and marguerites before netting and releasing. The doors are left open for ventilation when it's warm and we close them before night. I go over

The Greenhouse

to shut up the greenhouse when garden work is done for the day, ambling along, taking in the small changes in the borders. On a June evening before supper, I have one of those clear moments that make it all worthwhile. A song thrush sings from the top of our roof after the rain has stopped. A blackbird fledgling is newly out on a branch of the viburnum. The heron stands stock still in the field and a curlew calls flutingly over the hill.

Looking after the Vegetable Garden

Our Vegetable Garden is about the size of a traditional British allotment. Its four large beds, bisected by two paths to echo the Flower Garden, allow for rotating crops to prevent the build-up of pests and diseases. David keeps a record of the layout from year to year so that he can change the areas where each is grown. There are no permanent crops except for the strawberries, and these too are replaced from runners and moved to new soil every third year. All the home-made compost goes to enrich this area, the priority because it gives us food.

Years back at Chesters, my son Tom had noticed a large box shrub growing in the shelter belt of woodland that protected the walled garden. This was the species plant, *Buxus sempervirens*, and we found it tougher than the low box hedges of 'Suffruticosa' that edged the Chesters flower beds and is easily damaged by wheelbarrows or children running about. We took a mass of cuttings from this – about 1,000 – and rooted them on sand beds under a misting unit. Potted on, many went out for sale in the nursery, but they were also laid out as hedges around a series of vegetable beds. I felt quite attached to these and did not want to leave them behind. Digging them up was quite a job, but we tried to keep the hedges in sections so that they would be easy to replant. If the individual plants got detached from each other, it would be a jigsaw to put them back together again. Thankfully, we had some long trough-like plastic carriers and were able to transport the hedges in metre-long parts.

A long box hedge was the first element that went into the derelict ground that was destined to be the Vegetable Garden.

It created a boundary between the veg patch and a working area for cold frame, nursery bed and wheelbarrow store. With some spare box, David laid out two short and staggered hedges at 90 degrees to it so that they would break up the wind coming from the west. These are cut annually in about August so that their neat profile gives a satisfying definition to this area in winter. The only downside of the box is that it harbours slugs. At the end of the long box hedge and next to the path into the Vegetable Garden, I formed a topiary shape in variegated box, a cube topped with a pyramid to echo the two yews in the Flower Garden. Although the eye does not see such repetitions in the same view, it adds to the cohesion that unites the front and back areas. A single path, all in the same honey-coloured gravel, runs from alongside the woodland border at the front, down past the house, and forms the central path in the Vegetable Garden, an important design link between the two. The Flower Garden borders, with their asymmetric layout, are then echoed in reverse in the Vegetable Garden; longer on one side than the other. When viewing subtle devices like this, it's not immediately obvious why, but there is a unity and calm that is soothing.

The path drops down a couple of steps and beneath a rose arch. It meets the cross path – this one is of grass – at an offset central diamond, then ducks under another arch to end at a bench by the back garden wall. Here, we can sit with the sound of the river just behind us and a rectangle of chamomile for our feet, its apple scent drifting up to mingle with a pair of roses either side. Generally, roses do not do well in this garden but these two, pink 'Olivia Rose Austin', named after rose breeder David Austin's grandchild, have remained healthy.

Either side of this central path, we grow annuals, experimenting each year with different varieties. I don't bother with any that have had their nectar parts bred out in the drive for showy doubles, choosing instead only those of benefit to pollinators. Some of the best over the years have been the zinnias, the mix of bright colours in 'Molotov Mix' for example attracting hoverflies and butterflies, the scarlet flax 'Red Robin', which is a dazzling crimson, and old-fashioned candytuft. I sowed the candytuft ten years ago using a 50p packet of seed from an online seed specialist that does not use picture envelopes. Ever since, it has naturally regenerated, making a soft haze along the path in shades of white, pink and purple, attracting small skippers, *Thymelicus sylvestris*, flighty little butterflies with gleaming orange-brown wings that skip between the flowers.

I'm particularly fond of poppies. Some years, I might grow the old variety 'Shirley poppy' named after Shirley in Croydon. Now part of Greater London, it was a hamlet in the nineteenth century, and the variety was bred from field poppies by the then vicar, the Reverend William Wilkes, who had noticed one that had a narrow border of white in his garden. The flowers come in soft shades of white, salmon, lilac, apricot and deep pink with a characteristic white centre. Other years, it's been the strikingly patterned 'Danish Flag' with fringed scarlet petals and bright white centres, or 'Ladybird' rounded red petals and black centres, or I've cooled it all down with 'Bridal White'. Sometimes the seeds are scattered by the gales far away from the domed capsules with unusual results; a red field poppy blooming amongst the dissected fronds of royal fern. These are the shorter poppies, so behind them I will plant taller opium poppies, again trying out different varieties each year. There's been 'Pink Fizz' – bicoloured, ragged-edged petals -, 'Album' – palest lilac – and 'Hungarian Blue', which has become my favourite not so much for its crumpled deep violet flowers but for its glaucous and shapely seedpods.

Tucked into the front of these borders there are nasturtiums, low growing varieties such as 'Empress of India' with its deep dark leaves and scarlet flowers. When I smell nasturtium leaves, I am straight back in my childhood garden where I was allowed to grow them in a border in front of a wooden greenhouse. The vivid flowers would scramble about, fat stems twirling and curling as chunky seeds developed on their tips. Every year, they would be decimated by the dark green and yellow caterpillars of large white butterflies. Giving a child their own bit of garden to grow things in is a way of seeing nature and giving a sense of belonging. Those were my nasturtiums, grown by me. That peppery mustard smell of the leaves is one of my Proustian moments, like the scent of pinks or of ripe plums, immediately linking me back to decades before.

These annual borders either side of the path have a few permanent features, useful in winter when there's nothing else to see. All these are arranged in flanking pairs: aromatic *Artemisia camphorata* with its strong scent of camphor and leaves like finely cut southernwood, rhythmically leaved evergreen hebes that I took as cuttings from a roadside plant, and the low level variegated leaves of *Lamium* 'White Nancy', a spotted deadnettle with white flowers. Then there's more chamomile forming a wide green edging by the path that leads to the bench, the non-flowering 'Treneague', *Chamaemelum nobile* 'Treneague', a form that was found by botanist Dorothy Sewart in the 1930s at her home in Lower Treneague in Cornwall. Until then, all chamomile lawns needed constant mowing to take off their rangy flower stalks.

The two arches that emphasise the sight line down the path are made of willow. Sitting on the bench, with the river just over the wall behind, you can see through them right the way from the Vegetable Garden to the furthest wall of the Flower Garden, the widest span of the garden. One arch has a sprawl of golden hop clambering over it, bright yellow-green lobed leaves that turn golden yellow in autumn. Small cone-like hop flowers dangle down, this being a female plant (hops are dioecious with male and female flowers on separate plants). It's self-climbing so doesn't need any tying in and scrambles from ground level to the apex every year. I cut the old vines down in winter to allow for new growth.

The other arch carries a beautiful white rose that I bought as 'Little white pet', though I'm not sure that's the correct name. Sprays of semi-double small white roses cascade down from the willow framework, pale petals scattering onto the gravel path below. I planted it on the side of the prevailing westerlies so that it naturally wanted to grow over the curved roof. Initially, we made this arch from hazel coppiced from a nearby wood and used a template laid out on the ground, short posts around which we bent the bean poles. It was durable and lasted for some years but took quite a long time to make. We now use willow, allowing it to root so that it is anchored against the gales, flexing and bending with the wind.

During the growing season, I prune off any long shoots of willow but leave just enough so as not to stop it growing. It is formed of double hoops spaced a metre apart with two more hoops set crossways for bracing. These are bound at the top, and against a blue sky resemble the shape of a vaulted roof. Side sections of willow or hazel are lashed to the hoops at intervals forming ladders, everything bound together using tarred twine. If the arch gets damaged, it is easy to replace the willow rods using material from trees along the riverbank in the next field. This was planted as a revetment by the North Pennines National Landscape to stop erosion using willow stakes interwoven with lengths of willow that David and I helped to make as volunteers. Now it provides nest sites for willow warblers and osiers for us to harvest for garden structures.

The wooden-edged diamond at the centre of the Vegetable Garden has a sumptuously dark red 'William Shakespeare' rose rising out of lavender 'Hidcote' and a mass of *Allium aflatuense*. It's a bit lopsided because I once walked backwards into it whilst manoeuvring a wheelbarrow, painful for me and damaging for the rose. The diamond is the anchor at the centre of the four vegetable beds. Around it grows our food, the order and the neat lines a contrast to the exuberant planting of the Flower Garden.

When I need a sense of calm and order, I like to wander in the Vegetable Garden. It is restorative and that can be needed. In Beth Chatto's *Green Tapestry*, she writes, "Gardeners rarely become bored, but even the most enthusiastic of us become exhausted from time to time, not just physically but emotionally and mentally as well." Gardening can play tricks with the mind. I can look at what feels like perfection one moment and wake up the next morning and feel that the planting is out of control. It doesn't take much for it tip into chaos, especially the style of gardening that I embrace. All those self-seeders, the free-flowing run of one plant into another, the wildflowers and the meadow emulators can so easily run riot and be hard to bring back from the brink. Left unmanaged, it would very quickly become too wild, and it is that constant balancing act that I think makes it so poignant and so moving. Gardening unlike painting or another form of art – and I do think of it as art – is a complex mix of time, movement, light and seasons. It's a series of forever shifting relationships and this ephemeral nature, an awareness that it could be all be blown to the wind like a dandelion clock, is what makes it so eloquent.

It is David who produces the vegetables, sows seed and looks after this area of the garden. He rotates the crops to prevent the build up of disease, and we don't grow much fruit because it would take up a permanent space. But there are the essential strawberries for summer feasts and jam as well as Japanese wineberry, *Rubus phoenicolasius*, as this can be grown against a wall. In a dry corner, we grow the silver leaves and fulsome flower heads of globe artichokes, and a south-facing border is filled with herbs – the insect magnets that are marjorams, thymes and sages. Some herbs get cut back during the season to promote fresh growth that is usable for cooking such as chives, fennel and marjoram. We can get several harvests during the season from cutting back chives, though I leave some flowers for the bees. As well as the usual purple chives, there are two beautiful cultivars, both of which originated at Poynztfield Herbs Nursery near Inverness – 'Black Isle Blush', white flowers with pink centres, and 'Pink Perfection', a pure pink. Then there are three mounds of silver curry plant, clipped so that they can be seen from the larder window in an echo of a ceramic ball that stands on the terrace. By linking one thing with another, vistas and rhythmns are created that bring cohesion to the garden.

Along the western edge of the Vegetable Garden, we've planted a damson tree, an apple called 'Winston' that is suitable for this area, a hebe grown from a cutting in my aunt's garden and a flowering cherry, its fragile single pink flowers glorious against an April sky. There's a large bird cherry that sucks up moisture so the soil is no good for veg, but it does provide the dry ground that enables us to grow rosemary in this frost hollow. Here too are gladioli for cutting, annual cut flowers and a line of dahlia 'Bishop's children' grown from seed and that have survived five winters in the ground. Bee-friendly comfrey is grown in a triangular border next to the compost bins so that it can handily be cropped several times a year for adding feed and activation to the layers of compost. A working area covered in woodchip is a place for a cold frame, a wooden-edged seed bed and a raised bed for herbs. The path to the compost is edged in lavender and box domes, giving a visual link to the front and the small formal elements that help to anchor the wild abundance that is the Flower Garden.

Looking after the Flower Garden

Maintaining the Flower Garden is more complex as it is always evolving. The plants have a determination of their own, ebbing out from their original positions, seeding themselves and creating unplanned associations. It's a dynamic, constantly changing system. I have to work at maintaining a balance, refining and editing or getting tough. As when writing it is sometimes hard to let go of a favourite phrase that doesn't work in the text, so it is tempting in the garden to hang on to a plant that no longer contributes positively to the whole. It can take David or a friend to question its rightness in that spot. It probably stems from my days of running Chesters Walled Garden and not wanting to get rid of a possibly useful stock plant.

I always feel that the gardening year begins in late autumn. This is when changes can be made, plants dug up and moved around, bulbs planted, and as I garden I am visualising what it will look like in spring. Autumn work sets the scene for spring. Winters in Allendale are variable but they can be hard. Snow can lie for weeks, frost may not lift for many days. When the Beast from the East came in early March 2018, drifting snow reached the roof on some farmhouses higher up the East Allen valley. I may not be able to do anything in the garden for some weeks so I have learnt how much to cut back before winter and how much I can leave for the benefit of wildlife. I want to look out of the windows to see snow or frost on seedheads and the outlines of stems. I want to leave tall cardoons and grasses as lookout posts for robins, seedheads of thistle plants for birds to feed on and grasses for their rustling sound effects. I equally don't want to be struggling to catch up in late winter, wrestling with heavy, soggy foliage or being late in clearing the ground for bulbs to come up.

So I cut back much of the woodland border in autumn in readiness for snowdrops, snowflakes, crocuses and winter aconites. Because these emerge so early, this border takes priority. Heaps of leaves fall from the line of mature sycamores, blown by westerlies to lie against the wooden edging boards of paths or collect on the terraces. Enjoying the meditative repetition of raking, I gather them all up as a harvest and lay them across the woodland border to rot down naturally or be folded into the soil by worms. Just as the garden acts as a calendar for the year beginning with this border, I work from west to east in a gradual cut back. It is all part of the seasonal wave and I imagine a time-lapse film showing the rising and falling across the entirety of the Flower Garden.

Hardy geraniums are cut back midsummer to allow them to regrow and maybe re-flower. In late autumn, they are cut down a second time, the soft leafy growth perfect for composting. These are plants that would otherwise collapse into unattractive wetness and would then be difficult to cut with shears. I also cut back the notorious self-seeders, beginning with the willowherbs as they finish flowering. I grow two cultivars of rosebay willowherb, the delicately bi-coloured *Chamaenerion angustifolium* 'Isobel', which has softly pale pink petals with deeper pink star-shaped sepals showing between them. It's a much less aggressive plant than the species and it also spreads less than the other that I grow, the stately and serene white rosebay willowherb, *Chamaenerion angustifolium* 'Album'. How invasive it is will depend on position and soil, but I didn't realise this until a couple of years into being here. Where it grew at Chesters, in dry compacted earth and hemmed in by an arbour and a wall, it stayed within its allotted space. Once liberated into the newly turned soil of the Flower Garden, it romped away, sending out long deep roots to work their way into the crowns of other plants. It amuses me to see online sales describing it as not nearly as invasive as the wild plant and difficult to propagate.

Bees and other insects are attracted to its slender spires of pure white flowers on tall stems. Set at the back of the border, I can see it beyond the thinner white spires of *Veronicastrum virginicum* 'Album', a peaceful pairing of similar shapes that are distinct enough to make it interesting. Flowering in August and lasting for over six weeks, the white is set off by the deep green of trees outside the garden walls. Some say that the seed pods are sterile, others offer the seed for sale. Either way, I take no chances with willowherbs so I deadhead it as soon as I see the pods starting to expand and let loose their fluffy contents. Do this on a sunny day and they explode as you try and manoeuvre them into the wheelbarrow; choose a damp morning and they can be cut back without this risk. I then leave the willowherb stems minus the flowering tops well into autumn, especially as I grow it, apart from its beauty, because it is the food plant of the elephant hawk-moth caterpillar, *Deilephila elpenor*.

The autumn cutting back process is gradual, selecting anything that doesn't look good anymore, weighing up if it adds or detracts from the overall view. All plants reach a tipping point where they are better out of the picture until the next year. To begin with, we used to cart everything off to the compost heaps, chopping or shredding the woodier stems, which is time consuming. I've now combined this with the need to mulch the Flower Garden, making use of this great mass of material in situ. Petrol hedge trimmers have proved to be the most efficient way of reducing all the tall woody stalks to mulch. Cutting horizontally, the stems can be sliced in swathes, four inches at a time, until taken back to ground level. Here, they make a weed-suppressing sterile mulch, slowly rotting down underneath. So long as this fresh mulch is not mixed in with the soil but merely left on top, there should not be a nitrogen check. Leaves of monocotyledonous plants such as crocosmias make a particularly effective mulch, forming a thick, fibrous mat across the surface.

We have tried various mulches in the past fourteen years, depending on what's available, but the principle remains the same: cover the soil so that weeds cannot grow and keep moisture in during dry weather. It would be impossible to water the sizeable Flower Garden but, thanks to the mulch, it has managed perfectly well through over two months without rain. For a couple of years, we covered the ground in spent hops from the local brewery. Collecting them in large bags, they were heavy and wet to manage. Once out of the bags the hops could be easily spread with a rake, which was satisfying, but in dry conditions the wind would lift them across the paths and, when very wet, the crowns of some of the plants developed mould.

Woodchip proved to be a better mulch, much better for walking on when I was going to pick cut flowers from the borders. Driving home one day, I noticed the high-sided trailer belonging to a tree surgeon and stopped to ask if I could have the woodchip, the result of felling a large beech tree. The usual recommendation is to compost woodchip for over a year before applying it to the garden. When fresh woodchip is laid on the soil, fast reproducing bacteria works to break it down but it needs nitrogen to function. It will temporarily take this from the soil but once the decomposition process is over, the nitrogen returns to the soil as the bacteria die off. Providing the wood is just sitting on top of the surface, the bacteria will be working in a very fine layer and won't affect plants around it. After all, in a woodland situation, there is much fallen timber and this doesn't prevent ferns and woodland plants from thriving. For two years now, I've used fresh woodchip to no ill effect. There have been some spectacular showings of woodland fungi such as *Tubaria furfuracea* and *Ramaria stricta* as they work to break down the wood, a reminder that when sourcing wood-chip from a tree surgeon, you should check that the timber has not been infected with honey fungus, *Armillaria mellea*.

The plants that I allow to stay will be quick, brittle and light to cut back in February, making way for new growth and a new year. These are the stems and spent heads that look most interesting in winter. Snow or frost settles on the spiked balls of cardoons, their strong, ridged stems still standing against the winds and rising above drooping silver foliage. Bugbane, *Actaea racemosa*, its white heady scent long gone, is reduced to a ladder of flower stalks. The branches of tall *Euphorbia palustris* become swept upwards in a clasping bowl-like shape, a different attitude to the more outward burgeoning of summer. Drifts of bergamot are now dark brown angular stems topped in whorls of bristly domes. I've learnt too to look for visual joys and to value certain plant associations. The branched tops of sweet rocket, an evening-scented, invaluable plant for moths, turns pale beige against a dark background of nut brown asters.

The seedheads of wild carrot fold inwards, creating a cupped nest for spiders and insects. Sea hollies are a thorny, protected winter home for invertebrates. Leaving these plants during the cold months provides sanctuary for wildlife and patterns and structure for us to look at or for me to photograph. I see no value, though, in waiting til spring to cut back many of the lower story plants that slump into a soggy mess and become harder work for being left. Cutting down and mulching can benefit wildlife. Chopping up the hollow stems of plants such as milky bellflower, *Campanula lactiflora*, to leave them on the surface multiplies many times the tubes that provide hiding places for insects such as ladybirds. Lying horizontally, they don't get filled with water as would cut stems standing upright. They are dry, safe, hidden places to overwinter.

The sedums that grow either side of the path to the front door change throughout the year, from the humorously cabbage-like shapes of spring through summer when they quietly expand before becoming softly jade green, then pale pink topped, then rich pink before burgundy and winter brown. There's just a short period in February when they are cut back and there is not much to see, otherwise they are constantly evolving, ever interesting. It's a job I do at the same time as the grasses, part of the year's ritual and the seasonal events that give it shape.

I leave all the grasses until February, their buff and straw colours blending with the surrounding landscape, their repeated shapes giving rhythm across the border. Grass seedheads gleam with water drops or curl under frost. My favourite grass, *Hakonocloea macra*, grows to either side of the steps to the Flower Garden, cascading in dynamic umber forms. This only starts to disintegrate in late winter. It is then cut down to the base along with the cool season grasses. Ornamental grasses fall into two categories: grasses from cool climates and those from warm climates. It's the former that I cut back in early February, leaving grasses such as miscanthus until mid-spring. It depends a bit on the weather and how hard the winter has been. In some years, there is new growth sprouting through last season's stems and then it is time to cut down the calamagrostis, which I planted in a waving line through the perennials of the largest border of the Flower Garden. I chop up the pale biscuit-coloured stems to add to the mulch, being careful not to stand on any emerging daffodils.

Golden oats grass, *Stipa gigantea*, has its flower stems pruned back into the centre of the clump. I always wear goggles for this in case of poking my eye out on a sharp upright stem. It's a fiddly job that requires patience and is not something to do in a hurry, so I try and enjoy the slow mindful way of tracing each stem back inside the mound of foliage. I check the basal leaves of the clump itself for hibernating hedgehogs – they create the perfect thatched roof – before teasing out the dead foliage using a springbok rake. I find this much easier than using gloves and it is a satisfying process, thinning and clearing and leaving a swirl of glaucous green leaves. The pampas grass, *Cortaderia richardii*, is tackled similarly as I trace each flower stem back into the clump using lightweight loppers or good secateurs and always wearing goggles. The leaf blades have sharp edges so gloves are a must, and I take out the lower browned leaves to tidy it up. This pampas seeds easily – this clump in fact is only here because I had noticed a two-bladed tiny seedling at Chesters – so I look around for any that can be potted up. Years back, people used to burn pampas grass to remove the old growth and I remember someone setting fire to a clump with dramatic and rather scary results. It's not really recommended though because it can damage the crown of the plant.

As February turns into March, I know that I have a few weeks in which to get the Flower Garden thoroughly weeded. After that, the free-flowing way that it is planted means that it is harder to get between the interlocking growth. It's that top growth that in turn suppresses weeds as light cannot get to ground level and allow germination. The exception is of the many trees seeds: bird cherry, sycamore, ash, hawthorn. I like to focus on one particular weed – at this time of year, that is bitter cress – and to concentrate on it as I work through the borders. In terms of seeding, bitter cress is not even an annual, it's an ephemeral. That means that it can complete its life cycle from germination to flower to setting seed several times in a year, which is why it is important to break that process by weeding it out early on.

The other weed that I hunt down in early spring is broad-leaved willowherb, *Epilobium montanum*, a perennial with pink flowers and wind-borne seeds that can form spreading patches if I miss seeing it between other plants. Though it is a food plant for small phoenix and hawk-moths, I don't want it in the flower borders but am happy for it to be in wilder parts of the garden. Dandelions arrive on the wind from the fields outside, as does the spear thistle, though this is an easy and satisfying one to pull up with its taproot. Learning to distinguish seedlings is vital to my kind of gardening when there are generous plants that I want to nurture: verbascum, sweet rocket, perfoliate alexanders, honesty, Bowles' golden grass, corncockle and viper's bugloss. These seed themselves, often around the edges of the garden where the mulch is less deep, and then I will move them into places where I can imagine the later effect.

The walled garden at Chesters had a cocktail of the some of the most difficult weeds to eradicate, predating my tenure with many of them anchored in the fastness of retaining walls. I'd beat them back but they would re-emerge. As I ran the garden organically, they had to be managed as best as possible with constant vigilance for the curling stems of bindweed, the exploratory roots of ground elder or the easily broken white roots of enchanter's nightshade. Digging up clumps of peonies, irises, asters and other long-lived perennials, enough to fill two and a half horsebox loads, it's remarkable that we managed – with extreme care – not to bring along any of these invasive perennial weeds. The nettles that were already here were easy enough to dig out because they form thick mats of roots, their rich yellow colour an easy giveaway. Being next to farmland, the typical weeds are dock, plantain, deadnettle, chickweed and woundwort, some useful as herbs when growing in the right place. There was also couch grass, wrapped around muddy stones and one to thoroughly get rid of before the new plants went in. When digging, you have to make sure you pick out even small fragments of this forceful grass, which is called "wicken" in Northumberland, an apt name if it derives from wicked. When doing finer work, the best kneeling mat I have is an old Landrover bench seat from a scrapyard, three inches deep, covered in tough fabric and wide enough to shuffle along without having to get up.

I aim to have the garden weeded by April or May. After that, it becomes an unstoppable force as wave after wave of plants swell and flower. I will still move some plants about, providing I can hold their root balls together. Puddling in was a technique I learnt as a child from following around an old gardener and watching what he was doing. I fill the planting hole with water, replant and press down the soil to keep the water close to the roots. You learn over the years what you can get away with, some such as Brunnera tolerating being moved even in dry weather.

On the edge of the woodland border is a massive specimen of a rhubarb from Tibet that I was originally given from the National Trust herb garden of Acorn Bank in Cumbria. It was much photographed at Chesters, rising tall in the main herb border and inspiring artists and printmakers with its gunnera-like leaves and head-high plumes of pink flowers. Every year, its massive leaves are filigreed by dock beetles, *Gastrophysa viridula*, who lay their orange eggs on the underside of the foliage. If you try and catch these beautiful jewelled beetles, they will curl up their legs and drop instantly, falling to the ground or rolling like a pea into the centre of a leaf. As an organic gardener, I have learnt to live with the dock beetles and rather than squashing their eggs, I will cut back the rhubarb when it becomes a skeleton of midribs and veins.

Two years ago in mid-summer, I realised I could have a second wave once the rhubarb was gone by underplanting it with variegated brunnera. With its pretty marbled leaves, this is a plant that looks its best in autumn when lots of other plants in the woodland border have lost their foliage interest. I dug up a clump and pulled it apart, replanting a dozen rooted pieces where there was no longer shade from the rhubarb. After an initial watering, I left them – in very dry conditions – and they have thrived, now giving a second flush and bringing an entirely different leaf pattern to this area of the garden.

Over the years, I have had a number of volunteers, eager to learn about gardening and to work in this beautiful spot. Pegge from America wrote me an email afterwards in which she item-ised what she called "Susie's best practices". These were: one thing at a time (concentrate on one type of weed); don't give space to a plant that isn't working for you; puddle in new plants; allow plants to grow and mingle; and watch where you put your feet. She said she was much less destructive in her garden now that she had learnt to plant her feet and not move around so much. By growing plants closely together and as interlinked communities in this garden, I have to be careful not to damage them as I go through the borders. Looking ahead before choosing a spot to stand or crouch, I enjoy the yoga-like stretches needed to reach out to prune or weed.

Celebrating Place

With living and gardening here, I notice how the bowl of the hills captures a certain quality of light. It can be Mediterranean in its summer intensity, bouncing off the gravel on a blue sky day, rendering petals translucent. There's a clarity to the air, something to do with the way light is held in the palm of the valley. In contrast, there are six weeks in winter when the sun only just touches the house walls. Yet by spring, I am once again looking for shaded places to sit. I celebrate these contrasts and the incredible setting in which our house sits.

It is the evenings that are revelatory. This is when sunlight comes slanting in under the branches of the sycamores, backlighting the plants of the woodland border, making stained glass colours of hellebore petals, of foxglove and peony. The transformation can happen in a moment. The low angle of the sun slides in beneath the leaf canopy, shines through the line of trunks along the western boundary, glances over the stone wall and through the glowing flowers. It lasts for an hour or two perhaps, beautiful for being fleeting, until the light drops and the magic is gone.

Working in the borders, my focus is naturally close and it takes special times to draw back and see the larger whole. I get this also when I come back from being away, even if that has just been for an afternoon. There's a moment when, as I look over the main gate, I almost see the garden and the place through someone else's eyes. It's only then that I can see its beauty. Maybe this is because I am not looking for things that need to be done but am seeing the full picture for once. This also happens when I take photographs to go with my magazine articles or when people come to visit and I see their reactions.

In 2013, just three years after making the garden from scratch, a production team came from *BBC Gardeners' World* to film for the programme. They had seen the two-year series in *The English Garden* magazine and a researcher came in advance on a recce. Filming with presenter Joe Swift, I showed how the design of the garden linked to the landscape and explained the two guiding principles in its planting and the joy of experimenting through the lack of a planting plan. The programme went out the following March.

That same week in August when *Gardeners' World* was filmed, *The English Garden* sent the photographer Allan Pollok-Morris to record how it all looked in the year following the series in the magazine. Enchanted by the place, he stayed two and half days, waking before dawn to catch the sunrise, working through heavy rain to capture evocative shots of poetic atmosphere. In 2020, garden photographer Clive Nicholls took a dreamy and magical set of images, including them in his book *Brilliant British Gardens*. The garden is firmly private and I have to regularly say a polite no to requests from groups to visit. The way that I share it with people is through giving talks or in what I write, in particular through the double-page spread that I write every week for seven months of the year for *My Weekly* magazine. I began the column in 2014 so have been writing it now for ten years. I take all the photographs, describing to readers what is happening in the Flower Garden and the Vegetable Garden. With so much self-seeding, the planting is always shifting and changing. This brings new and often unexpected plant combinations, so the whole process is one of discovery and experimentation.

The *Country Diary* that I write for *The Guardian* is often inspired by something that I witness in the garden as well as in the surrounding land. The chocolate mining bees by the compost heap, moths from the night's trapping, dock beetles, garden fungi, hedgehogs, owlets, slow worms and tadpoles have all provided plenty to describe. A partridge making a nest in the thickets of the deepest part of the Flower Garden emerged with twelve camouflage-patterned fluffy chicks. A woodcock feather gave me material for making a drawing as well as the basis for my *Country Diary*.

Finding a centipede when turning over a clay pot gave me the opportunity to celebrate my uncle E.H. Eason who wrote what is still the definitive work, *Centipedes of the British Isles*. Elected a fellow of the Linnaean Society, he drew meticulous illustrations of centipedes, his archive and collections now held at the Oxford University Museum of Natural History. When a British centipede was identified by him as a separate species, it was named *Geophilus easoni* in his honour. In my student days, I spent one summer working on his Cotswold farm, glimpsing the book-lined study where my uncle would be engrossed in drawing and making notes. I would help on the farm in the mornings, my afternoons free to wander.

This high escarpment of Gloucestershire is an area of oolitic limestone, characterised by the honey-coloured walls that bound its fields. It is also rich in fossils. Walking the fields, I would spot them lying on the surface, turned up by ploughing, often well preserved. In a dusty gateway, pocked by the feet of sheep in winter and now dried out, a perfect plump fossil of a sea urchin. In a nearby quarry, a dinosaur had been found, a fabrosaurus, estimated to have lived between 167 and 164 million years ago. Finding centipedes in my garden always reminds me of my uncle and takes me back to that hot summer, just as flower scents or textures are an instant memory link to the past. Insects, birds, plants in my small meadow, they all are small events in the natural world of my garden that become pieces for my *Guardian* diaries.

The most remarkable diary is one from 2023. Woodcock are elusive, secretive birds so I was astonished when I saw one on the terrace close by our house. It was late May. That evening I watched it from a window as it preened and stretched its wings before flying off to the woods. It was clearly nesting in the narrow terrace border behind some irises and I was able to study it daily from the house, learning its movements. Utterly silent (in contrast to the noisy mallard that was at the time nesting in the Flower Garden) the woodcock would slip in and out between the foliage leaving no visible trace. It was so intent on nesting, or perhaps used to our movements, that it remained on the nest as we filled watering cans or mowed the lawn. Before we realised she was there, we had even had a cup of tea on the bench just a couple of metres away.

A female woodcock will nest on the ground and typically incubate her eggs for about three weeks. Within a few hours of hatching she will lead them away. I was rewarded for the many times that I had kept watch by being able to witness that fleeting and special moment. I noticed her sitting on the edge of the flower bed, plumped up, well camouflaged against a mottled background of seedheads fallen from the nearby sallow. When she stood up, there beneath her were four chicks, dappled tan and umber with diminutive woodcock beaks. It was a very moving moment and I felt anxious for them, protective of the chicks and feeling connection with them. To have a nesting woodcock seemed to me the ultimate assurance that we have made a garden that is beautiful for us to look at but is also to the benefit of wildlife. That I could write about it in my Country Diary was a way of sharing the moment.

Another way of celebrating all the abundance of beauty is to walk around the garden making up a bunch of flowers. The bouquet that I hold in my hands is a distillation of all that's good, of the flowers that are out in that particular moment. I've learnt which plants will last well in water without needing conditioning, ideally picking in the first part of the morning but often from necessity breaking the rules and gathering by evening too. I make the bunch up as I am walking round, starting with a handful of greenery such as lime green lady's mantle or greeny-brown bupleurum. Stripping the bottom leaves off as I go, I toss these onto the border or tuck them behind a clump. With the greenery held gently and openly in my left hand, I rotate it whilst poking into it the June stems of catmint, melancholy thistle, allium, knapweed and dianthus, ox-eye daisy, cephalaria, pink-flowered sage and roses.

As the season changes, the colours of the cut flowers change. An autumn bunch becomes an explosion of burning colours as orange heleniums, purple echinacea, Joe Pye weed and biscuity grasses jostle with pink cosmos. There's something to pick at any time of the year, with scented viburnum, hazel catkins and Algerian iris in the middle of winter. Some are plants that I dry, hanging up bunches of lavender 'Hidcote' in the subdued light of the larder or the annual strawflowers, *Helichrysum*, cheerful and papery in red, orange or pink.

Sometimes I invite friends who are artists to spend an afternoon drawing in the garden. It is exciting to see this thing that we have created through the eyes of photographers, painters or printmakers. And a visit by poet Linda France led to her writing *Bernard and Cerinthe*, which won the Poetry Society's National Poetry Competition in 2013. Sheltering from the rain in the greenhouse, she encountered the curious dusky flowers of *Cerinthe major* for the first time. She writes on the Poetry Society's website,

> *I remember very particularly the day I wrote this poem, actually. I went to visit a friend of mine who has the most beautiful garden. It was the end of August and there was a*

*plant I'd never seen before: cerinthe major 'Purpurascens',
and I was just astonished by it. It's a very intense blue and
the leaves are a silvery green...they're quite thick, almost
waxy, fleshy. That's one of the things I'm drawn to about
plants, they express this tremendous "otherness", but they
just stay there and let you respond to them, unlike a bird or
animal that disappears...*

The act of creation is a thread that has run through my life
whether it is making a garden or a drawing, experimenting with
natural dyes, weaving, woodwork, taking photographs or painting. When I left school my parents wanted me to learn to type
and to get a reliable job. I wanted to go to art school. After a
short spell of typing – it has now become very useful for com-
puter work – I didn't give up on my dream and was accepted at
the Ruskin School of Drawing at Oxford, now known as The
Ruskin School of Art. This art school in the 1970s was a place
of change, a tense dynamic between traditional skills of watercolour painting or drawing from plaster casts of Greek statues
in the Ashmolean Museum and experimental multi-media
abstract work. One of the visiting tutors was painter and sculp-
tor Maggi Hambling and once Duncan Grant came, wheeled in
in a wicker bath chair.

It's sad that filmmakers have portrayed John Ruskin in such
a one-sided way. He was far-sighted, thinking way ahead of his
time, a polymath, critic, social reformer, naturalist, plant scientist
and superb artist. He defended J.M.W. Turner's work at a time
when it was not understood. He promoted the Pre-Raphaelites,
was deeply concerned about pollution, was interested in art,
architecture, geology, horticulture and land management. Though
he wouldn't have used the word, he was an early ecologist and –
incredibly – he foresaw climate change.

Ruskin made a mountainside garden around his home of Brantwood on a hillside above Coniston Water in the Lake District. With its sublime views to the Old Man of Coniston and Wetherlam, it's a place I've visited many times. We even once stayed in the Eyrie, a self-catering apartment looking down onto the lake, next to the turret room with its lamp hanging in the window. Overnight, I was allowed to study one of Ruskin's water-colours of mosses on a rock, with his writing of "Brantwood 1875" in its right-hand corner. I had been making drawings of moss on bark and felt a strange connection with the person who had set up the art school where I had been taught. In the evenings when the visitors had left, we were able to wander in the garden.

There are eight separate gardens, some new, some historical. Around the slate-built Ruskin's Seat is the Professor's Garden, his favourite area dedicated to plants that are good for body and soul. The Moorland Garden, now outgrown, was the site of his visionary experiment in upland agriculture with terracing following the natural land form. More recently, during her time as Head Gardener at Brantwood, Sally Beamish created the allegorical Zig-Zaggy using Ruskin's sketched design. Idiosyncratic and experimental, it represents Dante's Purgatorial Mount on the passage of the soul from hell to paradise, and plants are chosen on each terrace according to the seven deadly sins. Paths zig-zag up through show-off plants symbolising pride or fruit trees for gluttony. Unusual mulches include charred wood, slate and sheep's wool. Having ascended the mountain, you reach the seven graces – among them kindness, humility, charity – to help on the soul's journey to paradise. Here, the path comes out into the gentler green spaces of the hillside with its trees, mosses and ferns.

The 250-acre Brantwood estate runs from the lakeshore up to the high fell. These woods on the steep slope are semi-natural, their coppice products used on a green wood course that I went on in 2012 just after we had started on our garden and were using local wood in its making. On display in the house are some of Ruskin's paintings, my favourite being his enormous brown ink drawing of unfurling horse chestnut leaves. Ruskin produced the most exquisite watercolours of the natural world as well as of architecture, his paintings of Venice full of light and air and magic.

At the Ruskin School of Drawing, I shared a studio with painter Jeremy Morgan – now known as Jeremy P.H. Morgan – and I can still visualise his paintings of the land, of clouds moving over windy hillsides. From up in this high studio above the Examination Schools, I used a Box Brownie, picked up in a jumble sale, to take photographs of the rooftops of Oxford. This cube-shaped basic camera made by Eastman Kodak uses a simple meniscus lens and projects an inverted image onto light-sensitive film at the back of the box. I saw an extraordinary demonstration of how this works when staying in a cottage in the Alpujarra of Spain. There, a small hole in the old wooden shutters projected an upside-down image of the church with its bell tower on to the blue wall of the bedroom. I loved this pinhole quality of the black and white images of the Box Brownie and would take it with me when I went down the High Street to Oxford Botanic Garden, the oldest botanic garden in the UK and one that has been there for 400 years.

I'd leave behind the traffic heading for Magdalen Bridge to go through the gate next to the pedimented and honey-coloured stone of the Danby Arch. It was the gateway into a magical walled garden, much as the key turned the lock in the heavy old door at Chesters. There, I first encountered the crazy corkscrew hazel that I now grow in my own garden, and I made drawings of the huge Amazonian lily pads in the glasshouses in the exotic moist air. I enjoyed the taxonomic beds for their order and system and visually accidental pairings of foliage and flowers, planted not with an idea of aesthetics but because they were in a particular botanical family. Perhaps in some way it influenced my wanting to collect, label and exhibit specimens of herbs. In summer, students would pass by in punts along the Cherwell. In winter, I'd sit on a bench in the furthest reach of the garden with a robin eating from my hand.

One time – and it is so clear in my memory that I can still experience it – I stopped on the High Street outside the botanic garden to listen to a blackbird singing. Liquid and fluting, clear and musical, it rooted me and I couldn't move, the song of the blackbird cutting through and floating above the sounds of cars and buses. There are many places that are overlaid by my memories of natural events. In Northumberland, I navigate by landmarks that are no longer there. I've lived here for so long, walked its footpaths, driven along its lanes, that my mental map is filled with ephemera. Wildlife encounters or vanished flowers exist still in my mind and mark these places. The bend where a leaping deer nearly crashed into my car. The bog in Kielder Forest where I found the elusive chickweed wintergreen. A hollow oak where wild bees nested near my house or the roadside post of a short-eared owl on moors near Scots Gap. The early purple orchid on a shady bank that I saw one year but not again and that I still look for every spring. When talking to the local farmer, we'll refer to a spot on the track as "black rabbit cattle grid". We both know exactly what we mean though it's now some ten years since the melanistic rabbit was seen there.

Local names, names that are not on any map, landmark trees, memories of events, these are all things that connect me to the place where I live. I enjoy celebrating that connection through art, from the smallest details to the wider landscape. My sketchbook pages contain cones from the Scots Pines by the river – drawn at different stages of their opening – alongside moss, beetles, ferns and rock faces. When my grandchildren visit, we sit outdoors drawing heron and goose feathers as I try to encourage them to look before putting pencil to paper. My own early drawing skills came from copying birds or animals in books. So much school or nursery teaching is not about studying or looking.

I carry my phone with me all the time as it is the most immediate way of capturing what I see. It's not one that is very up-to-date but the camera is good enough that many of the images are reproduced in magazines. It's also invaluable for taking quick photos of moths when I go through the moth trap, or of insects, wildflowers or spiders and anything that I want to identify later. Though there are identification apps, I enjoy the process of having to work out where a particular flower or insect fits within the genera. It is something that I learn from. Many of the photographs are used for social media, and always having my phone to hand means I can capture sudden effects of light in the garden. These are moments that I might otherwise miss if I had to go and fetch my proper camera. Creativeness moves on and it would have been hard to imagine how immediate and responsive the technology would become. And how different it will be for my grandchildren and for the naturalists and gardeners of the future.

Future Gardeners

I feel I have been incredibly lucky to have gardened all my life, to have been able to make it my career as well as my passion. Gardening led to my appreciation and study of the natural world. Many children grow up never having dug up potatoes or harvested carrots and without knowing the names of birds or flowers. The teams on the BBC's *University Challenge* can answer questions on quantum physics or astronomy but frequently don't know the names of plants, of British snakes or mammals. Thanks to my son growing up with an awareness of the natural world, my young grandchildren are making drawings not of generic birds but of golden eagles and curlews with their different shaped beaks. What I learnt and passed on, he is also passing on. Break this chain and it is very hard to regain.

I had an outdoor childhood in a garden with wild edges. Unhappy at school and often not very happy at home, I spent as much time as possible outside, wandering down overgrown lanes, crossing the railway line to where I had my thinking tree. Then, there were more corners of unused land, places where rusty bedsteads and buckled galvanised buckets lay covered in brambles, where sprawling ivy made dark thickets up elm trees. Our house had two orchards of apples and plums, with everything recorded in an orchard book that listed each tree grown in the Little Orchard and the Big Orchard. The handwritten notes in the book are of grease bands, fallen branches and numbers of bushels in the yearly crop. The gnarled trees fascinated me. One, a huge outgrown espalier, was over 100 years old and suitable for climbing. There were white painted numbers on the trees that linked to records in the book, old varieties such as Peasgood's Nonsuch, Bauman's Reinette, Ashmead's Kernel.

Daffodils grew in sweeping drifts between the fruit trees, giving way as the season moved on to ox-eye daisies in long grass when I would sling a hammock between the trees. When autumn came, we would pick the apples to fill wooden bushel boxes before taking them to the cellar where they would be laid on tall slatted apple racks, making sure the fruits did not touch. Stored for winter, we would still be eating them in pies and tarts by January or February. A wonderful variety of differently coloured apples hung above my head. I think of the words of Dylan Thomas in *Fern Hill*, "Down the rivers of the windfall light".

A couple of local men would come with an Allen Scythe to give the meadow an annual cut. This heavy, noisy piece of machinery had a wide-toothed blade that scissored back and forth against a fixed knife bed and large green painted iron wheels. It was dangerous and could run away with you, but it scythed easily through the three-foot-tall grass. All was then raked up into piles of sweet-smelling hay that could be used for bedding for our hens. Mint grew wild in one special spot, the perfumed variety known as *eau-de-cologne* mint. Grass snakes would slither through the meadow, sometimes coming out onto the lawn. A traumatic childhood moment for me was seeing someone kill a grass snake, chopping it behind the head, driven by fear but perhaps without understanding that it was harmless. As a child, I knew this was wrong.

There's a black and white photograph of me aged about three, trying to dig in a border by the house using a full-size garden fork, a look of intense concentration on my face. My father stands next to me, his hands hanging down by his sides. There's an energy to the photograph, a sense that he wants to help me but knows he must let me try to manage by myself to discover what I am capable of. Behind me is an ivy-covered brick wall at the base of which are the thin arching leaves of an iris. This was the first botanical name that I learned without realising it. My mother called it *Iris stylosa* and I liked the sound of that name so I copied it. Years later, I learnt that *stylosa* meant nib-shaped and that it refers to the coiled pointed flower buds of this, the Algerian iris. The name has now changed to *Iris peduncularis*, not half so memorable, poetic or expressive, and I'm sure I would not have imbibed that name as a child. It's a plant that I now grow at the base of the south-facing wall of our house. Here, it gets the bone-dry, summer-hot conditions that it needs, especially to flower well here in Northumberland, and it is a reference to those childhood plants.

The garden where I grew up had flower borders and vegetables, a fruit cage and annuals, but what I loved most of all were the wild corners. I knew where the tallest snowdrops could be found in a spinney, where muted coloured primroses grew in the grass. I was happy out in the garden, following around my parents' elderly gardener, Ern, learning from watching how he did things. Ernest Cox (he even had the name of an apple) had lived in the small hamlet all his life. He knew few plant names, but what he gave me was an instinctive feeling of how to garden. When I was a toddler, he would push me round in an old red painted wooden wheelbarrow. When I was a bit older, he would let me help to plant out or sow. He saved vegetable seeds, with clay pots in the greenhouse holding runner beans for next year; black mottled patterns on red kidney-shaped seeds. Cucumbers were trained along beneath the roof glass so that the fruits hung down; a glut would see my mother making a delicious cucumber soup that was served hot. One time, Ern set fire to the greenhouse and the fire brigade was called out – it was from one of the roll-ups that he always smoked.

I learnt how to cut or lay hedges, and to take my first cuttings of rosemary. Ern and I would stand in the orchard, feasting on sun-warm Victoria plums or noticing the frogs that clustered beneath the tap of the water butt. One time, we watched fireflies, glow-worm beetles, on a summer's evening, yellow-green points of light amongst the trees. Our family would have Sunday walks, a time to pick sloes to make into sloe gin or to find flowers to press and identify. My mother took me to Gilbert White's house, the Wakes, down sunken lanes and past the beech hangars that he wrote about in *The Natural History of Selborne*.

The front garden of Ern's brick semi-detached house, with its rows of bedding plants and bright annuals, had an unusual edging to the flower beds that particularly fascinated me. Post-war enamel signs, red lettering on white, warned of unexploded bombs. He had got them from a nearby army base and simply made use of them, all the way either side of the path to his front door. Writing about this made me look at his house on StreetView. His front garden, once colourful with flowers and visited by bees, had all been paved over. There was not a gap for even the smallest weed to put down its roots.

It is this attitude to the natural world that makes me want to share my knowledge and skills, and to pass them on to my grandchildren or to the people I have taught to garden. Every year at Chesters Walled Garden for a couple of summer weeks, we would have students on placement from school. Meeting some of them now, they say that it was one of the happiest times in their school career. My children would spend time after school in the walled garden, helping with potting up or weeding, or climbing into a leafy lilac to spy, hidden from the visiting public. Later, they would work in the shop and nursery, learning the names of the many herbs that we sold. My son thought that a dock plant was called a "doctor plant" because it alleviated nettle stings when rubbed onto skin. I sent in this story to Richard Mabey who was compiling information for the *Flora Britannica*, a huge contemporary flora of the cultural use of plants, a book of living folklore. Another story I submitted was about an elderly friend who fed the birds on her terrace. Noticing a four-foot-tall and handsome plant of cannabis, grown from spilt bird seed, I told her what it was. She rushed out to cut it down because she had the vicar and several ladies of the church coming to tea.

My children went to a small local first school where nature was included on the agenda. There was a competition to see who could bring in the tallest weed, a butterfly garden next to the playground, tadpoles reared in a tank and a nature table. Drawing is a valuable way of connecting with nature, the peaceful and mindful act of observation being the most important thing; the process rather than the result. Studying what we see can also be a way of overcoming fear. Since a child, I had been scared of spiders, especially the large house spiders, *Tegenaria gigantea*, that would come out at night or scrabble to get out of the bath. This persisted for years until I went on a field trip led by spider expert, Fran Garcia. Through discovering the different species and being swept along by the enthusiasm of the teacher, I gradually started learning more and found that being able to identify and classify them eased the fear. Now I can look at a house spider and note if it is male or female; males have large palps, appendages near their mouthparts. Being more analytical about something we are afraid of helps to provide a bit of mental distance, to even find spiders intriguing.

As my grandchildren pick strawberries or eat peas straight from the pod, dig potatoes or push around a small wheelbarrow, I hope that they are learning to be future gardeners. The garden is a great teacher. Through it, we find out about the cycles of growth and learn about life and death. And by looking to nature to inspire and influence how we garden, we can draw down a small part of the natural world. What David and I have created here in Allendale is, as so many gardens are, ephemeral. It changes year to year as plants shift and move around. It exists so long as we work in it and I do not know what kind of life it will have beyond that. The future of this garden and of the wildlife of this small valley in the North Pennines is uncertain. Its life persists through my writing, through being able to show how to make a garden that celebrates and includes wildlife. I look up to the circling buzzard and feel alive in that moment.

> *This is what the buzzard sees. The steep bank of wood-land in the valley below. River winding through fields of round backed sheep. A rabbit on the stony track. Bank vole hurrying to safety in the dry-stone wall. The many shapes and textures of plants in a garden. The figure of a woman straightening, shading her eyes with the back of her hand and gazing up.*

Homage to a Gardener

There's a grainy black-and-white photo, taken in my parents' garden. In it, I am reaching up to hand a biscuit to Ern. He is wearing his familiar tweed jacket over a white shirt and dark tie. His other hand balances a cup of tea and my dad stands next to him. I can feel the admiration in the turn of my head, in my upward gaze.

I guess I was then about four and he was in his late sixties. Ern lived next door and had gardened this two acre patch for most of his life. My parents had moved out from London to a Berkshire hamlet; one of my first experiences of the countryside was to fall face down amongst nettles. That didn't stop me spending as much time as possible in the garden.

I trotted about after Ern as he weeded vegetables, tied up dahlias or chopped kindling for the winter woodshed. Sometimes he'd give me a ride in the wooden wheelbarrow but for most of the time, he would work and I'd watch – or invent games to tease him. I'd taunt him with "Look where I am now, Ern!" as I ran on newly worked earth amongst rows of onions. He'd mutter to my parents – with a twinkle in his eye – about what "that there Susie" had gone and done now.

Sometimes my parents would get in extra help, but their gardening would be more rough and ready. Ern would say "That there Bill, he's no gardener" and others would look ham-fisted beside him. I teased them too. One man threw down his trowel when I dumped a mass of muddy weeds on his head. I just thought it was very funny.

As Ern and I went about in our little kingdom, he taught me the feel of gardening, which is something that can't be expressed in books. Something to do with observation and with hard work at a slow-seeming pace. He didn't know many plant names and didn't need to. My mother taught me those. She planted herbaceous borders in natural-looking groups but he would infiltrate

179

them with straight lines of nemesias or calceolarias. He delighted in the bright flowers of dahlias and chrysanths that "made a good show" and in the controlled rows in the vegetable garden.

In the white-painted greenhouse, trays of bedding plants were lined up on wooden slats. Re-using old tomato boxes, Ern would layer them in leaf mould topped with finely sieved soil. I'd help separate the young plants, their white roots firmly fixed in layers of leaves from several autumns back. Clay pots were filled with runner beans, saved for next spring's crop, their purple blotched skins wrinkling as they dried out. Beneath the staging were stacks of clay pots, encrusted with cobwebs.

Cucumbers hung from the roof, my mother making them into a delicious soup. Their vines would turn dry and crackly in autumn. Ern smoked roll-ups, using a metal cigarette rolling machine that he kept in his jacket pocket. When he set fire to the greenhouse, that drama just added to my esteem.

Years blend in my memory and my childhood seems to have been lived outdoors. In spring I knew where the tallest snowdrops grew in a dense grove of hazel. The orchard was full of daffodils, followed by clouds of delicate Queen Anne's lace with orange tip butterflies on the wing. By summer the grasses grew long and Alf would mow them with an Allen scythe to make way for the apple harvest. Then the trees dripped with Victoria plums and Ern and I would eat them straight off the branch, sun-warmed and sweet.

All these things he taught me to love. Not the rule book techniques of gardening, but the feel of it. I wish he could know that I've spent my life in gardening, that the "'controlled chaos'" of my flower borders echoes the wilder parts of that childhood garden. That I've written books, observed wildlife, experimented with planting and loved the whole process. I wish I could say to him, as I did long ago in the onion rows, " Look where I am now, Ern!"

Useful Resources

Blom, Jinny, *The Thoughtful Gardener: An Intelligent Approach to Garden Design* (Quarto Publishing 2017)

Bloom: What Gardeners Grow. 600 Plants Chosen by the World's Greatest Plantspeople (Frances Lincoln 2023)

Chatto, Beth, *Beth Chatto's Green Tapestry Revisited* (Berry & Co. 2021)

Chatto, Beth, *The Beth Chatto Handbook* (The Beth Chatto Gardens)

Colwell, Mary, *Curlew Moon* (William Collins 2018)

Dunnett, Nigel, *Naturalistic Planting Design* (Filbert Press 2019)

Golden, James, *The View from Federal Twist* (Filbert Press 2021)

Jarman, Derek, *Derek Jarman's Garden* (Thames and Hudson 1995)

Lloyd, Karen, *North Country: An anthology of landscape and nature* (Saraband 2022)

Lloyd, Christopher, *The Well-tempered Gardener* (Hachette 2014)

Lloyd, Christopher, *Gardener Cook* (Frances Lincoln 2001)

Lloyd, Christopher and Beth Chatto, *Dear Friend and Gardener: Letters on Life and Gardening* (Frances Lincoln 2013)

Pearson, Dan, *Dig Delve*, Online garden magazine (digdelve.com)

Pearson, Dan, *Tokachi Millennium Forest: Pioneering a New Way of Gardening with Nature* (Filbert Press 2020)

Raven, Sarah, *Sarah Raven's A Year Full of Veg: A harvest for all seasons* (Bloomsbury 2023)

Reckless Gardener, Online gardening magazine (reckless-gardener.co.uk)

Strawbridge, Brigit, *Dancing with Bees* (Chelsea Green 2019)

Tree, Isabella, *Wilding* (Pan Macmillan 2018)

#wildflowerhour – Botanical Society of Britain and Ireland – social media posts every Sunday

Image Gallery

If you would like to see a gallery of photographs illustrating Susie White's garden, as described in these pages, please visit the gallery online by scanning the QR code below.

Acknowledgements

I'd like to thank the many people who helped to dig up and move plants from Chesters and to bring them to their new home. People who gave their time, support, and friendship and helped to make all this possible.

Thank you to Peter Armstrong for his skill with a digger and to the friends who helped to transform this bare patch of ground into a garden. To Barry and Eileen Heywood for their many trips to the dump, for shifting boulders and taking away the motorbike engines! To the two Dots, Dot Humble and Dot Holder, for turning up every week for a year to clear and dig and keep us cheerful. And to Pegge Bogle, Sarah Ford, Fran Garcia and Jen, Rosie Hudson, Kim Lewis, Robin Moss, Charlotte Reid, Tracy Walton and Jenny Wigston. To Tamsin Westhorpe for believing we could do it and to my children, Tom and Emma White. Thank you to the publishing team at Saraband and to Sara Hunt for being such a supportive and friendly editor.

Finally, and most of all, thank you to David for sharing all the ups and downs and for being the mainstay of this creative experiment in garden making.

About the Author

Susie White has loved gardening since she was a child, making it her career alongside other aspects of creativity: painting, drawing, photographing and pottery. She has written several gardening books and her work is regularly featured in magazines. Since 2011, she has contributed a Country Diary to *The Guardian* and has been the garden columnist for *My Weekly* magazine since 2014. The garden she has created with her husband, David Oakley, has a distinctive, natural style. It was featured on BBC *Gardeners' World* and is a hub for wildlife in the North Pennine valley where they live.

PHOTO: SHONA BRANIGAN